Test Yourself

Introduction to Financial Accounting

Ingrid R. Torsay
DeKalb College
Clarkston, GA

Contributing Editors

John Heher, C.P.A.
Norwalk Community Technical College
Norwalk, CT

Kathy Dunning, C.M.A., M.B.A.
University of Mobile
Mobile, AL

Marie Smith, M.S., C.P.A.
Central Texas College
Killeen, TX

NTC LearningWorks
a division of NTC Publishing Group
Lincolnwood, Illinois

Library of Congress Cataloging-in-Publication Data
is available from the Library of Congress.

I dedicate this book with fondness and appreciation to two individuals: Mr. Billie Ray Simpson, Department Head, retired, Business Administration Department, DeKalb College—who believed in me and gave me my start in teaching; and Michelle G. McGovern, scientist, teacher, daughter—whose happy heart gives me hope and whose boundless love honors me.

A *Test Yourself Books, Inc.* Project

Published by NTC Publishing Group
© 1997 NTC Publishing Group, 4255 West Touhy Avenue
Lincolnwood (Chicago), Illinois 60646-1975 U.S.A.

6 7 8 9 VL 0 9 8 7 6 5 4 3 2 1

Contents

Acknowledgments

I want to thank my former students at DeKalb College who challenged and rewarded me with their energy, spirit, dedication, and humor. You have been important teachers to me.

This book could not have been written without the support, encouragement, and patience of Mr. Fred Grayson of Test Yourself Books, Inc. I owe him a large measure of thanks.

Four colleagues at DeKalb College have been supportive to me: Florine ONeal, always willing and eager to filter and synthesize ideas; Lou Squyres, mentor and advocate extraordinaire; Anna May Castricone, champion of wellness and education; Barbara Jean Hall, peer consultant and artful coach. I thank each one—their enthusiasm has inspired me.

James J. Brooks, III, C.P.A., provided me with "real world" experience in accounting. I appreciate his kindness and patience.

Professor Michael Morrisey and Professor Mary Hovinga at the University of Alabama at Birmingham have been examples to me of excellence in teaching; I am grateful to them.

To Gabriella and Eugene Torsay, my parents, I am always grateful for instilling in me the love of learning, and for the love and sacrifice of bringing me to the wonderful United States, where educational opportunities abound. To Johanna Benjatschek, my godmother, I owe my heartfelt thanks for her laughter, encouragement, and love.

Special thanks go to several individuals whose care and support were very helpful so I could concentrate on my work: Dr. Mark Bashor and Katie Bashor, and their children Ryan and Jessie, who opened their home to me and fed me for two months; Sister Mary Jane Lubinski, O.P., who gave me a quiet place to work; Father John Adamski, who provided good counsel; Chris Kaylor, most loyal friend, who performed yeoman work in improving my writing; Virginia Soules, M.D.; Louise Collins, nurse; Barbara Denton, and Jennifer Chambers, neuromuscular therapist, who helped me feel well; Jacqueline Grant, M.D., good friend and occasional driver; Dennis McGovern, who took care of business with grace and humor; and Mr. Robert Kaiser of American Engineering Test in St. Paul, MN, who made office facilities available to me for the preparation of much of the first draft of this manuscript.

Preface

This book is designed to help students prepare for financial accounting exams. Better preparation can reduce the stress and anxiety so common to students before taking exams. These chapters have been written to complement your accounting textbook. In addition to studying textbook material, taking practice tests can enhance a student's performance on an examination given by an instructor. I have attempted to balance the material between theory and exercises. During my eleven years' teaching experience, I have found that students frequently overlook the material pertaining to theoretical concepts. This omission can be remedied with education and motivation, and I hope that this book makes a contribution to that objective.

Ingrid R. Torsay

How to Use this Book

This "Test Yourself" book is part of a unique series designed to help you improve your test scores on almost any type of examination you will face. Too often, you will study for a test—quiz, midterm, or final—and come away with a score that is lower than anticipated. Why? Because there is no way for you to really know how much you understand a topic until you've taken a test. The *purpose* of the test, after all, is to test your complete understanding of the material.

The "Test Yourself" series offers you a way to improve your scores and to actually test your knowledge at the time you use this book. Consider each chapter a diagnostic pretest in a specific topic. Answer the questions, check your answers, and then give yourself a grade. Then, and only then, will you know where your strengths and, more important, weaknesses are. Once these areas are identified, you can strategically focus your study on those topics that need additional work.

Each book in this series presents a specific subject in an organized manner, and although each "Test Yourself" chapter may not correspond to exactly the same chapter in your textbook, you should have little difficulty in locating the specific topic you are studying. Written by educators in the field, each book is designed to correspond, as much as possible, to the leading textbooks. This means that you can feel confident in using this book, and that regardless of your textbook, professor, or school, you will be much better prepared for anything you will encounter on your test.

Each chapter has four parts:

 Brief Yourself. All chapters contain a brief overview of the topic that is intended to give you a more thorough understanding of the material with which you need to be familiar. Sometimes this information is presented at the beginning of the chapter, and sometimes it flows throughout the chapter, to review your understanding of various *units* within the chapter.

 Test Yourself. Each chapter covers a specific topic corresponding to one that you will find in your textbook. Answer the questions, either on a separate page or directly in the book, if there is room.

 Check Yourself. Check your answers. Every question is fully answered and explained. These answers will be the key to your increased understanding. If you answered the question incorrectly, read the explanations to *learn* and *understand* the material. You will note that at the end of every answer you will be referred to a specific subtopic within that chapter, so you can focus your studying and prepare more efficiently.

 Grade Yourself. At the end of each chapter is a self-diagnostic key. By indicating on this form the numbers of those questions you answered incorrectly, you will have a clear picture of your weak areas.

There are no secrets to test success. Only good preparation can guarantee higher grades. By utilizing this "Test Yourself" book, you will have a better chance of improving your scores and understanding the subject more fully.

Introduction to Financial Accounting

Brief Yourself

Accounting is an information system. The goal of accounting is to communicate financial information about an organization to those who rely on that information for decision-making. The final product of financial accounting, the set of financial statements, reports the profitability of an organization, the changes in the owners' equity accounts, its financial health, and the changes in its cash flow. To achieve that end, an accounting system must first measure the effect of daily activity on the organization and then process and summarize the information.

The users of accounting information range from those with a direct financial interest in an organization, such as managers, investors, and creditors, to those with an indirect financial interest, such as taxing authorities, economic planners, and labor unions. Managers operate within an organization and have access to information not available to the remaining group of decision-makers, sometimes referred to as outsiders. Financial accounting emphasizes the information needs of these outside decision-makers. This is a major distinction between financial accounting and managerial accounting.

All organizations, for-profit and not-for-profit, must prepare accounting information. For-profit businesses are formed according to one of three models: sole proprietorships, partnerships, or corporations. Variations in accounting treatment result from these differences in the form of ownership.

Organizations differ by the nature of their operations. Some organizations—a physician's office, for example—render services. These are called service companies. Some other types of organizations buy and sell products; these are called merchandising companies. Still other types of organizations make the products they sell; these are called manufacturing companies. Variations in accounting treatment result from these differences in the nature of the operations.

For accounting information to be as useful as possible, the fundamental ground rule—or *matching principle*—must be established. The matching principle is implemented through the accrual basis of accounting. More will follow about this rule in a later chapter. Essentially, the rule states that the result of financial activity must be measured and recorded as it occurs; the financial activity occurs independently from the exchange of cash between parties.

Test Yourself

1. Choose the statement that provides the *best* modern definition of accounting.

   a. a system that measures, processes, and communicates financial information about an organization

   b. a system that maintains financial records

   c. a set of company books

   d. the computer system that furnishes financial information

2. Describe a major distinguishing characteristic of financial accounting.

3. A user of accounting information with a direct financial interest in the organization is:

   a. the Internal Revenue Service.

   b. a loan officer of a bank to which a loan application has been made.

   c. the Securities and Exchange Commission.

   d. an economic planner.

4. Which of the following users of accounting information has an indirect financial interest in an organization?

   a. a creditor of the organization

   b. a potential investor in the organization

   c. the labor union of workers of the organization

   d. management of the organization

5. Which organization currently holds the authority to prescribe *generally accepted accounting principles*?

   a. American Accounting Association

   b. American Institute of Certified Public Accountants

   c. Securities and Exchange Commission

   d. Financial Accounting Standards Board

6. On which financial statement would the words, "For the year ended..." not appear in the heading?

   a. Income Statement

   b. Statement of Owner's Equity

   c. Balance Sheet

   d. Statement of Cash Flows

7. Which financial statement represents the accounting equation, Assets = Liabilities + Owner's Equity?

   a. Income Statement

   b. Statement of Owner's Equity

   c. Balance Sheet

   d. Statement of Cash Flows

8. What does the income statement measure?

   a. liquidity

   b. solvency

   c. profitability

   d. resources

9. A company that makes auto parts and sells them to a national retail chain is a:

   a. merchandising company.

   b. manufacturing company.

   c. service company.

   d. partnership.

10. Which of the following forms of business organizations is considered a separate legal entity?

    a. sole proprietorship

    b. partnership

    c. corporation

    d. all of the above

11. Which of the following forms of business organizations is considered a separate accounting entity?

    a. sole proprietorship

    b. partnership

    c. corporation

    d. all of the above

12. Why is the cash balance at the end of the accounting period generally not equal to the net income?

Check Yourself

1. Answer (a) is correct because it is the *best* definition. Accounting is a system that measures, processes, and communicates financial information about an organization. Answer (b) describes bookkeeping, one aspect of accounting. Answers (c) and (d) describe components of an accounting system. (**Characteristics of accounting**)

2. The primary goal of financial accounting is to satisfy the information needs of the outside user of accounting information. Information is generated and reported according to generally accepted accounting principles in order to protect the outside users of the information. (**Characteristics of accounting**)

3. Answer (b) is correct. Creditors and potential creditors have a direct financial interest in the accounting information of an organization, since they risk their assets and suffer a loss when a poor decision is made. Answers (a), (c)), and (d) all have an *indirect* financial interest in an organization's accounting information. (**Users of accounting information**)

4. Answer (c) is correct. The labor union, which often negotiates on behalf of workers for wages and benefits, has an indirect interest in the accounting information of an organization. Answers (a), (b), and (d) are examples of groups and/or individuals with a direct financial interest in the accounting information of an organization. (**Users of accounting information**)

5. Answer (d) is correct. The Financial Accounting Standards Board invites comments from other organizations and professional practitioners. However, it has sole authority to set standards. The American Accounting Association (a) and the American Institute of Certified Public Accountants (b) are professional organizations. The Securities and Exchange Commission (c) is a regulatory agency. (**Financial reporting standards and practices**)

6. Answer (c) is correct. The balance sheet is concerned with the information at a point in time, as in a snapshot. The heading of the balance sheet indicates the date only. The other three statements provide information about activity for a period of time, as in a motion picture. These use the words "For the year (or month, etc.) ended ..." (**Financial reporting standards and practices**)

7. Answer (c) is correct. The foundation of the balance sheet is the accounting equation, Assets = Liabilities + Owner's Equity. (**Financial reporting standards and practices**)

8. Answer (c) is correct. The income statement measures profitability by reporting the difference between total revenues and total expenses. (**Financial reporting standards and practices**)

9. Answer (b) is correct. A manufacturing company is one that makes and sells its products. Answer (a) is incorrect because a merchandiser sells a product but does not make it. Answer (c) is incorrect because a service company renders a service and does not deal with selling products. Answer (d) is incorrect because it pertains to the legal form of a business, not to the nature of the operations. (**Types of business operations**)

10. Answer (c) is correct. A key characteristic of a corporation is that it is a separate legal entity from its owners. **(Legal form of business organizations)**

11. Answer (d) is correct. All business organizations are separate accounting entities; the financial records of the business and the owners must not be intermingled. **(Legal form of business organizations)**

12. The components of net income, revenues and expenses, are recognized when earned and incurred, respectively, and not dependent on the timing of the exchange of cash. Furthermore, the cash balance may be affected by non-income statement items, such as loans, investments, and withdrawals. **(Accrual basis of accounting)**

Grade Yourself

Circle the numbers of the questions you missed, then fill in the total incorrect for each topic. If you answered more than three questions incorrectly, you need to focus on that topic. (If a topic has less than three questions and you had at least one wrong, we suggest you study that topic also. Read your textbook, a review book, or ask your teacher for help.)

Subject: Introduction to Financial Accounting

Topic	Question Numbers	Number Incorrect
Characteristics of accounting	1, 2	
Users of accounting information	3, 4	
Financial reporting standards and practices	5, 6, 7, 8	
Types of business operations	9	
Legal form of business organizations	10, 11	
Accrual basis of accounting	12	

Analyzing and Recording Transactions: Preparing Financial Statements

2

Brief Yourself

Before accounting information is communicated, it is first recorded and summarized. Accountants today employ a system that has evolved from the work of a fifteenth-century Franciscan monk, Luca Pacioli. Basic terms and practices, described below, must be understood for the system to function effectively.

An *account* is the basic storage unit or classification for accounting data. Examples of accounts are cash, accounts payable, owner's capital, commissions earned, utility expenses, etc.

A *general ledger* is a book or file that contains all the individual accounts that the company uses. In a manual system, the general ledger contains at least one page for each account.

A *chart of accounts* acts as a table of contents for the general ledger. Each account contained in the general ledger is referenced with a number. The numbers are assigned in a series beginning with assets, then liabilities, capital, withdrawal, revenues, and expenses.

A *debit* is a number written on the *left* side of the account. A *credit* is a number written on the *right* side of the account. That's all! In accounting, contrary to popular usage, that's all that these words mean. We get the idea that a credit means an increase because, when our bank or credit union credits our account, our balance increases. Consider this, however: when a department store credits our account, our balance decreases. In the first example, credit meant an increase; in the second, credit meant a decrease.

How do we keep straight when to debit and when to credit? We follow the *rules of debit and credit*. Here's how those rules work.

The rules go back to the accounting equation and the process of analyzing the effect of a transaction on the components of the equation.

$$A = L + OE$$

Some transactions cause an asset to increase. An asset is on the *left* side of the accounting equation; the rule says, therefore, that an increase to an asset should be shown with a number written on the *left* or debit side of the account.

The rules also say that for every debit there must be a credit in an equal amount. This is what we mean when we refer to the *double-entry* system.

When we debit the asset account, how do we know which account to credit? That depends on why the asset increased.

Sometimes an asset increases because a liability increases, as when supplies are bought on credit. Liabilities fall on the *right* side of the accounting equation. To increase a liability, we need to write the amount on the *right* or credit side of the account.

When an asset increases because a liability increases, the asset is debited and the liability is credited.

Sometimes one asset increases because another asset decreases, as when cash is collected from a customer who owed us money as result of an earlier transaction. In that case, cash increased and accounts receivable decreased. We know that cash is debited because we show increases in assets (left side of the equation) as debits (left side of the account). Decreases in assets have to be shown in the opposite way from increases, so decrease to assets are shown with credits. When accounts receivable decreases, we credit that account.

A *journal* is a book in which transactions are recorded as they first occur. (Sometimes the journal is referred to as the *book of original entry*.) In a journal we will see the transactions for a company in chronological order. In a journal we see the entire transaction at a glance. That means we see the debit of a transaction on one line and then the credit side of the transaction in the very next line. This is different from the general ledger, where we see only the activity pertaining to one account at a glance.

A *general journal* is just one kind of journal, but it's the most basic kind. It uses two columns for the transaction amounts: one for the debits, and one for the credits.

A recorded transaction requiring more than one debit and/or more than one credit is a *compound journal entry*.

Posting is the process of transferring the data from the journal to the *general ledger*.

A *posting reference* is the key element in the cross-referencing system that leads you from the journal to the ledger, or from the ledger back to the journal.

In the journal, the posting reference we see is the *account number* used in the general ledger. In the ledger, the posting reference we see is the *journal page number* where the entry was first recorded.

A *trial balance* is a list of all the accounts with balances that a company uses at any given time. The order of the trial balance is the same as the order of the accounts in the general ledger. A trial balance has two columns for numbers, one for the debit balances, one for the credit balances. The purpose of the trial balance is to check that the general ledger is in balance before the financial statements are prepared.

Care must be taken not to mistake a trial balance for a balance sheet. A balance sheet is a formal financial statement that gives the status of a company's assets, liabilities, and owner's equity at a given time. It is *not* arranged in debit and credit columns. A trial balance is a worksheet that lists *all* the company's accounts. It is arranged according to debit and credit columns.

Test Yourself

Michelle Martin, a trained geologist, has established a new business called Environmental Testing Services. She advises contractors on soil conditions and provides testing services to determine levels of contaminants. She has asked you to help her *organize* her *financial information* and *develop* an *accounting system* that will lead to the *preparation of financial statements*. You want to do a good job because, although Michelle is starting out small, the need for this service is increasing. You want to be a part of this business success story.

1. From your initial interview with your new client, you want to identify for her some basic accounts she will need to use and their position in the Accounting Equation. In the space next to it, for each item place an *A* if it is an Asset, an *L* if it is a Liability, or a *C* if it affects *Capital*.

    a. Computer _____

    b. Note Payable _____

    c. Testing Equipment _____

    d. Cash _____

    e. Testing Fees Revenue _____

    f. Accounts Receivable _____

    g. Telephone Expense _____

    h. Michelle Martin, Withdrawal _____

2. Keeping in mind the position it occupies in the Accounting Equation, for each account indicate the *normal* or *usual balance* by placing in the space next to it **DR** for a *Debit* or **CR** for a *Credit*:

    a. Computer _____

    b. Note Payable _____

    c. Testing Equipment _____

    d. Cash _____

    e. Testing Fees Revenue _____

    f. Accounts Receivable _____

    g. Telephone Expense _____

    h. Michelle Martin, Withdrawal _____

3. For each account listed below, indicate what is required to show the change (increase or decrease) by placing **DR**, for a Debit, or **CR**, for a Credit, on the line beside it.

    a. an increase in Testing Equipment _____

    b. an increase in Note Payable _____

    c. a decrease in Accounts Receivable _____

    d. an increase in Testing Fees Revenue _____

    e. a decrease in Cash _____

    f. an increase in Telephone Expense _____

    g. an increase in Michelle Martin, Withdrawal _____

4. For each of the following items (a–i), create a T-account, and record the debit and the credit of each transaction. If an item is not a transaction, write out the words "no transaction." Be sure to mark each of the items in the T-accounts with a letter corresponding to the following items in order to identify these items more easily.

   a. Michelle officially began the business by opening up a business checking account with $1,000 of personal savings.

   b. Michelle purchased $5,000 of testing equipment by signing a note.

   c. Michelle transferred her brand new $3,500 personal computer to the business.

   d. Michelle scheduled a preliminary appointment with a contractor to discuss a potential $1,500 job.

   e. After her bid from (d) above was accepted, Michelle completed the work and billed the contractor for the $1,500 fee.

   f. A check from the contractor for $750 was received in the mail. The contractor promised to send the balance in two weeks.

   g. Michelle sent a check for $500 to cover her first 10% installment on the note she signed for the testing equipment (ignore interest).

   h. A $30 telephone bill from Southern Bell was received in the mail. It's not due until the fifteenth of next month, so Michelle is putting it in a folder marked "bills not yet due."

   i. Michelle withdrew $150 so she could make the payment on her student loan.

5. Prepare the transactions in Question 4 in general journal form.

6. Post the journal entries in Question 5 to the general ledger accounts provided.

7. Prepare a trial balance from the general ledger balances in Question 6.

8. Prepare an Income Statement, a Statement of Owner's Equity, and a Balance Sheet for Environmental Testing Services based on the trial balance in Question 7.

Check Yourself

1. a. A, b. L, c. A, d. A, e. C, f. A, g. C, h. C **(Classification of accounts)**

2. a. DR, b. CR, c. DR, d. DR, e. CR, f. DR, g. DR, h. DR **(Normal balance of an account)**

3. a. DR, b. CR, c. CR, d. CR, e. CR, f. DR, g. DR **(Rules of debit and credit)**

4.

	Cash				Accounts Payable				Michelle Martin, Capital	
a.	1,000	500	g.			30	h.		1,000	a.
f.	750	150	i.			<u>30</u>			3,500	c.
	<u>1,100</u>								<u>4,500</u>	

	Accounts Receivable				Note Payable				Michelle Martin, Withdrawal	
e.	1,500	750	f.	g.	500	5,000	g.	i.	150	
	<u>750</u>					<u>4,500</u>			<u>150</u>	

	Testing Equipment			Testing Fees Revenue	
b.	5,000				1,500	e.
	<u>5,000</u>				<u>1,500</u>	

	Computer Equipment			Telephone Expense	
c.	3,500		h.	30	
	<u>3,500</u>			30	

d. no transaction

(Recording transactions in T-accounts)

5.

Date	Account Name	Post. Ref.	Debit	Credit
a.	Cash Michelle Martin, Capital		1,000	1,000
b.	Testing Equipment Note Payable		5,000	5,000
c.	Computer Equipment Michelle Martin, Capital		3,500	3,500
d.	no transaction			
e.	Accounts Receivable Testing Fees Revenue		1,500	1,500
f.	Cash Accounts Receivable		750	750
g.	Note Payable Cash		500	500
h.	Telephone Expense Accounts Payable		30	30
i.	Michelle Martin, Withdrawal Cash		150	150

(Recording transactions in general journal form)

6.

CASH

Date	Description	Post. Ref.	Debit	Credit	Balance Debit	Balance Credit
a.		J1	1,000		1,000	
f.		J1	750		1,750	
g.		J1		500	1,250	
j.		J1		150	1,100	

ACCOUNTS RECEIVABLE

Date	Description	Post. Ref.	Debit	Credit	Balance Debit	Balance Credit
e.		J1	1,500		1,500	
f.		J1		750	750	

TESTING EQUIPMENT

Date	Description	Post. Ref.	Debit	Credit	Balance Debit	Balance Credit
b.		J1	5,000		5,000	

COMPUTER EQUIPMENT

Date	Description	Post. Ref.	Debit	Credit	Balance Debit	Balance Credit
c.		J1	3,500		3,500	

ACCOUNTS PAYABLE

Date	Description	Post. Ref.	Debit	Credit	Balance Debit	Balance Credit
h.		J1		30		30

6. (*continued*)

NOTE PAYABLE

Date	Description	Post. Ref.	Debit	Credit	Balance Debit	Balance Credit
b.		J1		5,000		5,000
g.		J1	500			4,500

MICHELLE MARTIN, CAPITAL

Date	Description	Post. Ref.	Debit	Credit	Balance Debit	Balance Credit
a.		J1		1,000		1,000
c.		J1		3,500		4,500

MICHELLE MARTIN, WITHDRAWAL

Date	Description	Post. Ref.	Debit	Credit	Balance Debit	Balance Credit
i.		J1	150		150	

TESTING FEES REVENUE

Date	Description	Post. Ref.	Debit	Credit	Balance Debit	Balance Credit
e.		J1		1,500		1,500

TELEPHONE EXPENSE

Date	Description	Post. Ref.	Debit	Credit	Balance Debit	Balance Credit
h.		J1	30		30	

(Posting from the general journal to the general ledger)

7.

Environmental Testing Services Trial Balance June 30, 19XX		
Account Name	Debit	Credit
Cash	$1,100	
Accounts Receivable	750	
Testing Equipment	5,000	
Computer Equipment	3,500	
Accounts Payable		$30
Notes Payable		4,500
Michelle Martin, Capital		4,500
Michelle Martin, Withdrawal	150	

(Preparing a trial balance from general ledger account balances)

8.

Environmental Testing Services
Income Statement
For the Month Ended June 30, 199X

Testing Fees Revenue	$1,500
Telephone Expense	30
Net Income	$1,470

Environmental Testing Services
Statement of Owner's Equity
For the Month Ended June 30, 199X

Michelle Martin, Capital, June 1, 199x		$0
Add: Investments by Michelle Martin	$4,500	
Net Income	1,470	5,970
Subtotal		$5,970
Less: Withdrawal		150
Michelle Martin, Capital, June 30, 199x		$5,820

8. (*continued*)

Environmental Testing Services
Balance Sheet
June 30, 19XX

Assets		Liabilities	
Cash	$1,100	Accounts Payable	$30
Accounts Receivable	750	Note Payable	4,500
Testing Equipment	5,000	Total Liabilities	4,530
Computer Equipment	3,500		
		Owner's Equity	
		Michelle Martin, Capital	$5,820
Total Assets	$10,350	Total Liabilities and Owner's Equity	$10,530

(Preparing financial statements from a trial balance)

Grade Yourself

Circle the numbers of the questions you missed, then fill in the total incorrect for each topic. If you answered more than three questions incorrectly, you need to focus on that topic. (If a topic has less than three questions and you had at least one wrong, we suggest you study that topic also. Read your textbook, a review book, or ask your teacher for help.)

Subject: Analyzing and Recording Transactions: Preparing Financial Statements

Topic	Question Numbers	Number Incorrect
Classification of accounts	1	
Normal balance of an account	2	
Rules of debit and credit	3	
Recording transactions in T-accounts	4	
Recording transactions in general journal form	5	
Posting from the general journal to the general ledger	6	
Preparing a trial balance from general ledger account balances	7	
Preparing financial statements from a trial balance	8	

Adjusting the Account Balances

3

Brief Yourself

This chapter examines adjusting entries — the reasons they are necessary and the mechanics that make them work. Hint: an understanding of Chapter 2 is essential before proceeding with this chapter.

The *matching rule* states that revenue must be assigned to the accounting period in which the goods were sold or the services were performed, and expenses must be assigned to the accounting period in which they were used to produce revenue. *Be careful not to confuse the matching rule with the double-entry system of accounting.*

Accrual-based accounting is an application of the matching rule. In other words, accountants record revenue in the period in which it was earned, not necessarily at the time the cash payment was received. Accountants also record expenses for the period to which they apply, not necessarily at the time of cash payment. Accountants demonstrate that they practice accrual accounting whenever they use the categories *accounts receivable* and *accounts payable*.

To further implement the matching rule, it is necessary for accountants to *adjust the accounts* periodically. The four types of situations that require adjusting entries are:

1. Costs benefiting future accounting periods have been paid in advance. These costs have been recorded, and need to be allocated to the proper accounting period(s).

2. Cash for services to be rendered in the future is collected in advance. This cash, received and recorded, must be allocated among the periods for which the earnings apply.

3. Earned revenues have not been recorded.

4. Incurred expenses have not been recorded.

The first two are examples of *deferrals*. The latter two are examples of *accruals*. *Every adjusting entry includes one balance sheet account and one income statement account.* Accordingly, failure to make the appropriate adjusting entry affects both the balance sheet and the income statement. For example, assets on the balance sheet can be overstated, and expenses on the income statement can be understated, thereby overstating net income. Careful reading and analysis are imperative in order to make the proper adjusting entry.

A *deferral* is the *postponement* of the *recognition* of an *expense already paid* or a *revenue already received*. For instance, an insurance premium paid in advance is charged to an asset, not to an expense. So the recognition of the expense is postponed until the time elapses. Then the adjustment takes care of shifting the amount to expense. Deferral adjusting entries fall into two types: 1) adjust between assets and expenses; and 2) adjust between liabilities (unearned revenues) and revenues.

An *accrual* is the *recognition* of an *expense or revenue* that has arisen but *has not yet been recorded*. The adjusting entry takes care of recording what has taken place. For instance, say your company's payday is every Friday. Wage expense is normally recorded on the books every payday (Friday). But if the cutoff date for your year-end occurs on a workday other than a Friday, you will have to make an accrual for the number of days' wage expense that has occurred since the last payday. If you neglect to make this accrual adjustment, you will leave out the wage expense for the partial week at the end of the year. Instead, the expense for the partial week will be charged to the succeeding year. The result is an understatement of Year 1 expense and an overstatement of Year 2 expense. Accrual adjusting entries fall into two types: 1) adjust between assets and revenues; and 2) adjust between expenses and liabilities.

A very important point to remember when preparing an adjustment entry is that *the adjustment represents the change* (increase or decrease) that is occurring in an account. Do *not* include the account's pre-existing balance in the adjustment. The objective of an adjustment is to add an amount or subtract an amount from an opening balance. Sometimes that opening balance is zero.

Depreciation requires a specific type of adjusting entry. It is used by organizations that have purchased long-term assets—plant and equipment, for example. The cost of plant and equipment is first charged to an asset account because its benefit will extend well into the future. As the company is enjoying the benefit of the use of that asset, its cost is gradually charged, or allocated, to expense. That process of allocating the cost of an asset, such as plant and equipment, to expense is called *depreciation*. The recording of depreciation is one example of a deferral adjusting entry. Recording depreciation expense is accomplished by the following:

> Depreciation expense xx
> Accumulated Depreciation xx

Accumulated depreciation is a *contra-asset* account. It has a balance opposite from the asset balance. So, accumulated depreciation has a normal credit balance.

The difference between the depreciation expense account and the accumulated depreciation account is significant and should not be overlooked because of the similarity of titles. The depreciation expense account contains only the current period depreciation, whereas the accumulated depreciation account stores all the depreciation taken on an asset from the beginning of its life with the company.

The depreciation expense balance is reported on the income statement; the accumulated depreciation balance is reported on the balance sheet.

The *adjusted trial balance* is a trial balance prepared after the adjusting entries are completed. New balances must be computed for those accounts that were adjusted. All accounts with balances, whether adjusted or not, must be included in the adjusted trial balance. The financial statements must be prepared based on the balances in the adjusted trial balance.

Test Yourself

1. The matching rule is implemented by using the:

    a. cash basis of accounting.

    b. accrual basis of accounting.

    c. double-entry system of bookkeeping.

    d. debit column and the credit column side-by-side.

2. Which one of the following statements is correct with respect to the accrual basis of accounting?

    a. The net income calculated is less meaningful than that calculated using the cash basis

    b. It results in higher net income than the cash basis

    c. It results in lower net income than the cash basis

    d. It is required by *Generally Accepted Accounting Principles*

3. Which of the following does not represent an application of the accrual basis of accounting?

    a. recognizing revenues when earned

    b. recognizing expenses as they help generate revenues

    c. waiting to record revenues when the customer makes a payment

    d. recording expenses when resources have expired

4. All of the following are valid reasons for adjusting accounts *except*:

    a. to allocate revenues earned and expenses incurred to the time period to which they pertain.

    b. to facilitate the comparability of financial statements.

    c. to calculate the correct balance in the cash account.

    d. to avoid the overstatement or understatement of assets.

5. Which of the following is true about a *contra* account?

    a. Its normal balance is opposite from the normal balance of its related account.

    b. It is reported on the financial statement as a subtraction from its related account.

    c. It always has a debit balance.

    d. Both (a) and (b) are correct.

6. All of the following accounts appear on the balance sheet *except*

    a. Building

    b. Depreciation Expense—Building

    c. Land

    d. Accumulated Depreciation — Building

7. *Real* accounts:

    a. are permanent.

    b. are temporary.

    c. may be reported on the income statement.

    d. begin with a zero balance each accounting period.

8. *Nominal* accounts:

    a. are permanent.

    b. are temporary.

    c. may be reported on the income statement.

    d. Both (b) and (c) are correct.

9. The *accounting* definition of depreciation is best described as:

    a. the decline in value of an asset.

    b. the obsolescence of an asset.

    c. the wearing away of an asset.

    d. the allocation of the cost of an asset.

10. Which underlying accounting principle mandates the depreciation of property, plant, and equipment?

    a. the matching rule

    b. the historical cost rule

    c. the conservatism rule

    d. the timeliness rule

11. Which of the following situations requires a deferral-type adjusting entry on December 31, 19X4, the year-end for Environmental Testing Services?

    a. The 8.5% 90-day note, made payable on November 1, 19X4, to Fulton Bank, is due on January 30, 19X5.

    b. A six-month advance payment for the rental of the suite of offices was made to Aranyi Leasing Company on July 1, 19X4.

    c. Clients were sent bills for work performed through December 15, 19X4. Since then, eighty additional hours of work have been performed.

    d. A new microscope, ordered one week earlier, is delivered by Package Deliveries, Inc.

12. Which of the following situations requires an accrual-type adjusting entry on December 31, 19X4, the year-end for Environmental Testing Services?

    a. The 90-day interest-bearing note, made payable on November 1, 19X4, to Fulton Bank, is due on January 30, 19X5.

    b. A six-month advance payment for the rental of the suite of offices was made to Aranyi Leasing Company on July 1, 19X4.

    c. The services guaranteed by advance payments from clients on October 1, 19X4, have been completed.

    d. A new microscope, ordered one week earlier, is delivered by Package Deliveries, Inc.

13. Which of the following pairs of accounts could not appear in the same adjusting journal entry?

    a. Office Salaries Expense and Office Salaries Payable

    b. Unearned Revenues and Revenues Earned

    c. Depreciation Expense and Accumulated Depreciation

    d. Interest Expense and Interest Receivable

14. The account Unearned Service Revenue is reported on the

    a. Balance Sheet as an Asset

    b. Balance Sheet as a Liability

    c. Income Statement as a Revenue

    d. Both (b) and (c) are correct

In each of the following situations, question numbers 15 through 17, choose the correct adjusting journal entry to be made on the books of Environmental Testing Services on *December 31, 19X4.*

15. On July 1, Environmental Testing Services made an advance payment for a six-month rental on its suite of offices.

    a. a debit to Rent Expense and a credit to Cash

    b. a debit to Rent Expense and a credit to Prepaid Rent

    c. a debit to Prepaid Rent and a credit to Cash

    d. a debit to Prepaid Rent and a credit to Rent Revenue

16. The services guaranteed by advance payments from clients on October 1, 19X4, have been completed.

    a. a debit to Unearned Service Revenue and a credit to Service Revenue Earned

    b. a debit to Cash and a credit to Service Revenue Earned

    c. a debit to Service Revenue Earned and a credit to Unearned Service Revenue

    d. a debit to Prepaid Service Revenue and a credit to Cash

17. Clients already were sent bills for work performed through December 15, 19X4. Since then, eighty additional hours of work have been performed.

    a. a debit to Cash and a credit to Accrued Fees Receivable

    b. a debit to Accrued Fees Receivable and a credit to Cash

    c. a debit to Accrued Fees Receivable and a credit to Service Revenue Earned

    d. a debit to Service Revenue Earned and a credit to Accrued Fees Receivable

18. When a recording error has been made and the entry has *not* been posted, which of the following procedures is the correct one to follow?

    a. erasing the incorrect entry

    b. ignoring the incorrect entry if the amount is insignificant

    c. preparing a new entry

    d. drawing a line through the incorrect entry and writing in the correct one

19. An adjusted trial balance is prepared in order to:

    a. help prepare the adjusting journal entries.

    b. check that the general ledger remained in balance following the adjusting entries.

    c. help prepare the financial statements.

    d. Both (b) and (c) are correct.

20. The order in which financial statements are prepared is:

    a. balance sheet, income statement, statement of owner's equity.

    b. income statement, balance sheet, statement of owner's equity.

    c. income statement, statement of owner's equity, balance sheet.

    d. All of the above are correct.

For each of the following oversights, state whether *total assets* will be understated, overstated, or not affected.

21. Failure to record expired rent

22. Failure to record accrued interest on a savings bond

23. Failure to record depreciation

24. Failure to record accrued wages

25. Failure to convert unearned revenue to earned revenue

26. Failure to record unbilled accrued fees earned.

For each of the following oversights, state whether *net income* will be understated or overstated.

27. Failure to record expired rent

28. Failure to record accrued interest on a savings bond

29. Failure to record depreciation

30. Failure to record accrued wages

31. Failure to convert unearned revenue to earned revenue

32. Failure to record unbilled accrued fees earned.

For each of the situations described below, provide the correct adjusting journal entry to be recorded on the books of Environmental Testing Services, on December 31, 19X4.

33. When office supplies for $700 had been purchased earlier in the year, the amount had been charged to the asset account Office Supplies. An inventory at year-end revealed that only $125 of supplies remained in the storage closet.

34. Depreciation for the year for a truck purchased in early January is estimated to be $3,600.

35. The weekly payroll amounts to $10,000 each Friday, the result of a five-day work week. December 31, 19X4, occurs on a Wednesday.

36. A twelve-month insurance policy costing $720 was purchased March 1.

37. Accrued interest on a note payable to Fulton Bank is $45.

38. All but $200 in services had been provided to a client who had made a $1,200 advance payment.

39. Referring to number 34 above, prepare the information in the form as it would appear on the balance sheet.

40. State how the accrual basis of accounting pertains to a magazine publishing company, and provide an example of an adjusting entry.

Check Yourself

1. b. Accrual basis allocates revenues to the accounting period in which they were earned and allocates expenses to the period in which the expenses led to generating revenues. (**The matching rule and the accrual basis of accounting**)

2. d. GAAP *does* require the accrual basis of accounting. Not (a) because net income calculated on the accrual basis allows for comparison from one accounting period to the next, thus more meaningful. Not (b) or (c) because accrual basis net income could be higher or lower than cash-basis net income. (**The matching rule and the accrual basis of accounting**)

3. c. Revenues are earned when, in the case of a service-type business, the service provider has completed rendering the service or, in the case of a merchandising or a manufacturing company, when the title to the product has shifted from the seller to the buyer. Collection of cash may or may not coincide with the earnings process. (**The matching rule and the accrual basis of accounting**)

4. c. Normally, the cash account is not adjusted during the formal adjusting entry process. (**The purpose of adjusting entries**)

5. d. Not (c) since some contra accounts have a debit balance and some have a credit balance—e.g., Sales Discounts has a debit balance and Accumulated Depreciation has a credit balance. (**The purpose of adjusting entries**)

6. b. Any depreciation expense account will appear on the income statement as a component of total expenses. *Hint: It is extremely important to distinguish between depreciation expense and accumulated depreciation.* The depreciation expense account reflects the depreciation for the current period only; hence, the heading on the income statement stating "for the year ended" or "for the month ended." As the name suggests, accumulated depreciation reflects all the depreciation since the beginning of the life of the asset. (**The purpose of adjusting entries**)

7. a. Real accounts are balance sheet accounts and carry forward period after period. (**The purpose of adjusting entries**)

8. d. Nominal accounts are accounts in name only; they actually are subsets of owner's capital and, thus, temporary. Most nominal accounts, revenues and expenses, are reported on the income statement. Only owner's withdrawal and income summary are not. (**The purpose of adjusting entries**)

9. d. Depreciation is the expired service potential of an asset. The cost is expensed in the period it contributed to the generation of revenue. The justification for depreciation is the matching rule. (**The purpose of adjusting entries**)

10. a. See number 9. (**The purpose of adjusting entries**)

11. b. Deferral-type adjustments are required when *a preceding cash exchange has occurred* and has been recorded, but the revenue process or the expense process followed later, i.e., was deferred. The deferral-type adjustment is the follow-up to the initial cash transaction. (a) and (c) are accrual-type; (d) is an original transaction. (**The purpose of adjusting entries**)

12. a. Accrual-type adjustments are used when revenue has been earned or when an expense has been incurred, but nothing has been recorded and *the cash exchange will follow*. In this case, it is important to distinguish between the note and the interest. (**The purpose of adjusting entries**)

13. d. In accrual-type adjustments, the account pairs are always assets and revenues, as in the case of interest receivable and interest income; or expenses and liabilities, as in the case of interest expense and interest payable. On the other hand, in deferral-type adjustments, the account pairs are always assets and expenses, as in the case of prepaid insurance and insurance expense; or liabilities and revenues, as in the case of unearned revenue and revenue earned. (**The purpose of adjusting entries**)

14. b. Unearned Revenue represents a future obligation of service for which cash already has been collected. (**The purpose of adjusting entries**)

15. b. Rent Expense is increased; the asset Prepaid Rent is decreased, since all of the prepayment has expired. (**The purpose of adjusting entries**)

16. a. The liability account is decreased, since the obligation has been satisfied; the revenue account is increased, since services have been rendered and the revenue has been earned. (**The purpose of adjusting entries**)

17. c. The asset account is increased to reflect the additional amount receivable; the revenue account is increased to reflect the additional earnings from services rendered since December 15. (**The purpose of adjusting entries**)

18. d. Not (a); erasures give the appearance of an attempt to conceal something. Not (b); estimates are allowed when it is not possible or practical to obtain precise information. In this case, the correct information is known and should be corrected. If the wrong amount has been posted to the correct account, the error can be corrected in the same manner. However, if the amount has been *posted to the wrong account*, a new entry, as in (c) is the correct procedure to follow. (**The purpose of adjusting entries**)

19. d. Not (a) because the adjustments precede the adjusted trial balance. (**The purpose of adjusting entries**)

20. c. Net income or net loss must be calculated first to show the effect on owner's capital in the statement of owner's equity; ending owner's capital must be calculated to be reported on the balance sheet, the ending date of the accounting period. *Hint: It is important to distinguish between the trial balance and the balance sheet.* The trial balance, in addition to being a work-sheet list of all the company's account balances, usually shows the owner's capital balance from the beginning of the period; whereas, the balance sheet, a formal financial statement, reports the ending balance in owner's capital. (**The purpose of adjusting entries**)

21. overstated: failure to decrease Prepaid Rent (**Failure to record adjusting entries**)

22. understated: failure to increase Interest Receivable (**Failure to record adjusting entries**)

23. overstated: failure to increase Accumulated Depreciation, resulting in failure to decrease the carrying value or net book value of the depreciable asset (**Failure to record adjusting entries**)

24. not affected: affects expenses and liabilities (**Failure to record adjusting entries**)

25. not affected: affects liabilities and revenues (**Failure to record adjusting entries**)

26. understated: failure to record accrued fees receivable **(Failure to record adjusting entries)**

27. overstated: failure to record rent expense **(Failure to record adjusting entries)**

28. understated: failure to record interest income **(Failure to record adjusting entries)**

29. overstated: failure to record depreciation expense **(Failure to record adjusting entries)**

30. overstated: failure to record wages expense **(Failure to record adjusting entries)**

31. understated: failure to record earned revenue **(Failure to record adjusting entries)**

32. understated: failure to record earned revenue **(Failure to record adjusting entries)**

33.

	DR	CR
Office Supplies Expense	575	
Office Supplies		575

Calculation: $700 Office Supplies Available

125 Ending Office Supplies on Hand

$575 Office Supplies Uses

(Adjusting journal entries)

34.

	DR	CR
Depreciation Expense — Truck	3,600	
Accumulated Depreciation — Truck		3,600

Calculation:

$$\frac{\text{Cost} - \text{Estimated Salvage Value}}{\text{Estimated Usefule Life}} = \frac{\$19,000 - \$1,000}{5 \text{years}} = \$3,600$$

(Adjusting journal entries)

35.

	DR	CR
Wage Expense	6,000	
Wages Payable		6,000

Calculation: $\dfrac{\$10,000}{5 \text{ days}} = \$2,000 \text{ per day}$

$2,000 per day @ 3 days (Monday, Tuesday, Wednesday) = $6,000

(Adjusting journal entries)

36.

	DR	CR
Insurance Expense	600	
Insurance Payable		600
Prepaid Insurance	600	

Calculation: $720 × 10 months/12 months = $600
(or $720/12 = $60 × 10 months = $600)

(Adjusting journal entries)

37.

	DR	CR
Interest Expense	45	
Interest Payable		45

(Adjusting journal entries)

38.

	DR	CR
Unearned Service Revenue	1,000	
Service Revenue Earned		1,000

Calculation: $1,200   Obligation from Advance Payment
             200   Unexpired Obligation at Year-end
           $1,000   Obligation Satisfied Through Earnings Process

(Adjusting journal entries)

39.

Environmental Testing Services
Balance Sheet
December 31, 19X4

Assets

Current Assets

Cash		$xx
Accounts Receivable		xx
Supplies		xx
Total Current Assets		xxx

Property, Plant, and Equipment

Truck	$19,000	
Less: Accumulated Depreciation — Truck	3,600	15,400
Total Assets		$xxxxxx

(Financial reporting)

40. The advance payment from subscribers received by a magazine publishing company results in an obligation to those subscribers; if the obligation exists at the balance sheet date, the amount is reported in the liability section of the balance sheet. The obligation, or liability, is satisfied as subscribers receive the publications as ordered. As fulfillment of the obligation occurs, the liability is reduced and the revenue earned is increased. This translates to an adjusting debit to the account Unearned Subscriptions Received in Advance (a liability account) and a credit to Subscription Revenue Earned. **(Explanation of adjusting entry)**

Grade Yourself

Circle the numbers of the questions you missed, then fill in the total incorrect for each topic. If you answered more than three questions incorrectly, you need to focus on that topic. (If a topic has less than three questions and you had at least one wrong, we suggest you study that topic also. Read your textbook, a review book, or ask your teacher for help.)

Subject: Adjusting the Account Balances

Topic	Question Numbers	Number Incorrect
The matching rule and the accrual basis of accounting	1, 2, 3	
The purpose of adjusting entries	4, 5, 6, 7, 8, 9, 10, 11, 12, 13, 14, 15, 16, 17, 18, 19, 20	
Failure to record adjusting entries	21, 22, 23, 24, 25, 26, 27, 28, 29, 30, 31, 32	
Adjusting journal entries	33, 34, 35, 36, 37, 38	
Financial reporting	39	
Explanation of adjusting entry	40	

Completing the Accounting Cycle

4

Brief Yourself

The content of this chapter turns our attention to the completion of the accounting cycle for a service company. Following a brief overview, we consider the completion of the ten-column worksheet, and then the preparation of the financial statements, the closing entries, and the post-closing trial balance.

The sequence of steps in the accounting cycle is:

    A. Analyze transactions from source documents.

    B. Record transactions in the journal.

    C. Post journal entries to the general ledger and prepare a trial balance.

    D. Make end-of-period adjustments, usually with the help of a worksheet.

    E. Prepare formal financial statements.

    F. Journalize and post closing entries.

    G. Journalize and post reversing entries.

The steps to prepare a worksheet are:

    A. Prepare the original trial balance (the one from the regular transactions) in columns 1 and 2 of the worksheet.

    B. Enter the adjustments into columns 3 and 4 of the worksheet, referencing each debit and its corresponding credit. Total the columns. It may be necessary to add additional account titles in the *Account Name* column.

    C. Enter the account balances in columns 5 and 6. The accounts that were adjusted will have new balances. Some accounts, which were not adjusted, such as cash, will contain the same balance as in the initial trial balance. Make sure the totals of the columns match before continuing to the next step.

D. Enter the balances from the adjusted trial balance columns, 5 and 6, to either the income statement columns, 7 and 8, or to the balance sheet columns, 9 and 10.

E. 1) Compute initial totals, sometimes called footings, for columns 7 through 10. These almost never match.

2) Compute the difference between the total of column 7 and the total of column 8; do the same for difference between columns 9 and 10. The difference between 7 and 8 should match the difference between 9 and 10.

3) Enter the difference between columns 7 and 8 on the side with the smaller amount. Enter the difference between columns 9 and 10 on the side with the smaller amount. If that difference appears in columns 7 and 10, then the company will report net income (the revenues, column 8, were more than the expenses, column 7); if that difference appears in columns 8 and 9, then the company experienced a net loss (the expenses, column 7, were more than the revenues, column 8).

4) Recompute the totals for columns 7 and 8, then for 9 and 10, by including the *differences* from the step above in the new totals. The new totals for 7 and 8 should now be identical; the new totals for 9 and 10 should now be identical.

The worksheet is an optional additional step that helps the accountant in three ways:

A. preparing the financial statements

B. recording the adjusting entries

C. recording the closing entries

The worksheet is not a substitute for any of the steps of the accounting cycle identified above. Instead, it is an additional tool for the accountant or bookkeeper.

A specific sequence must be followed in preparing the financial statements: first, the income statement, then the statement of owner's equity, and then the balance sheet. This is so because the amount of net income, or net loss, is used to determine the new ending balance in owner's capital. That balance, calculated in the statement of owner's equity, is used, in turn, on the balance sheet.

The adjusting entries that were prepared on the worksheet must be recorded formally in the journal and posted to the general ledger. The account balances in the general ledger are still the old, unadjusted amounts until somebody takes the time to record and post the adjustments. You want the general ledger to be right. Remember that the worksheet is not a substitute for the steps in the accounting cycle.

Closing entries are journal entries made at the end of the accounting period, after the financial statements have been prepared and the adjusting entries have been recorded in the journal and posted. *Closing entries are not at all the same as adjusting entries.*

Closing entries set all the temporary (nominal) account balances to zero. This is necessary so that the data pertaining to the revenues, expenses, and withdrawals of the accounting period just ended do not get mixed together with the data pertaining to the revenues, expenses, and withdrawals of the new period about to begin. The new period can then begin with a clean slate.

Closing entries also merge the result of the revenues, expenses, and withdrawals (those subsets of owner's capital) into the owner's capital balance, and will reflect the amount on the balance sheet.

The four closing entries are:

    A. Close *Revenue* accounts to *Income Summary*.

Revenues	xx	
Income Summary		xx

Debit each revenue account for exactly the amount of its credit balance; credit the temporary clearing account called Income Summary. This can be accomplished with one compound entry. Each revenue account will now have a zero balance.

    B. Close *Expense* accounts to *Income Summary*.

Income Summary	xx	
Expenses	xx	

Credit each expense account for exactly the amount of its debit balance; debit the temporary clearing account called Income Summary. This can be accomplished with one compound entry. Each expense account will now have a zero balance.

    C. Close *Income Summary* to *Owner's Capital*.

1) If revenues exceeded expenses, then:

Income Summary	xx	
Owner's Capital		xx

    OR

2) If expenses exceeded revenues, then:

Owner's Capital	xx	
Income Summary		xx

Do whatever it takes to set the Income Summary account balance to zero. If Income Summary has a credit balance, then debit it for the same amount; credit owner's capital for that amount also. You have just increased owner's capital by the amount of the net income.

Or, if Income Summary has a debit balance, then credit it for the same amount; debit owner's capital for that amount also. You have just decreased owner's capital by the amount of the net loss.

    D. Close *Withdrawals* to *Owner's Capital.*

Owner's Capital	xx
Withdrawals	xx

Credit the owner's withdrawal account for exactly the amount of its debit balance; debit the owner's capital account for that amount, too. You have just decreased the owner's capital account by the amount of his/her withdrawals.

A Post-Closing Trial Balance is a trial balance prepared after the closing entries have been recorded and posted.

Only balance sheet (real) accounts should appear in the post-closing trial balance, because all the other accounts the company uses are temporary and should have zero balances at this point. If a temporary account appears in the post-closing trial balance, then something went wrong with the closing entries and should be fixed.

Preparing reversing entries is an optional step on the first day of the new accounting period. Only the accrual-type adjusting entries may be reversed. Reversing entries make the succeeding entries pertaining to the accrual adjusting entries simpler for the bookkeeper. To prepare a reversing entry, simply transpose the accrual-type adjusting journal entry.

Test Yourself

1. Each of the following actions represents a step in the accounting cycle. Place one number—from 1 to 5—next to each action to show its correct position with respect to other steps in the accounting cycle.

   _____ Prepare the financial statements.

   _____ Prepare the ten-column worksheet.

   _____ Analyze the source document.

   _____ Post to the general ledger.

   _____ Record the entry in the journal.

2. Which of the following statements does not describe one of the purposes in preparing the ten-column worksheet?

   a. assist in analyzing the source documents

   b. assist in preparing the closing entries

   c. assist in preparing the financial statements

   d. assist in preparing the adjusting entries

3. Which of the following items would not appear on a completed ten-column worksheet?

   a. Accumulated Depreciation — Equipment

   b. Michelle Martin, Capital, beginning balance

   c. Michelle Martin, Capital, ending balance

   d. Michelle Martin, Withdrawal

4. Which columns on the ten-column worksheet would be out of balance after the initial footing?

   a. the trial balance columns

   b. the adjustments column

   c. the income statement and balance sheet columns

   d. All columns should be in balance all the time

5. If a net loss occurs, where does the amount appear on the ten-column worksheet?

   a. on the credit side of the Income Statement columns

   b. on the credit side of the Balance Sheet columns

   c. on the debit side of the Balance Sheet columns

   d. Both (a) and (c) are correct

6. Each of the following categories represents a pair of columns in the ten-column worksheet. Place one number—from 1 to 5—next to each category to show its correct position with respect to other categories on the worksheet.

   _____ Adjusted Trial Balance

   _____ Balance Sheet

   _____ Trial Balance

   _____ Adjustments

   _____ Income Statement

7. Complete the Adjustments columns in the worksheet below from the information provided.

   a. The Prepaid Insurance represents an eighteen-month policy purchased in early January 19X5.

   b. The Prepaid Rent has expired.

   c. An inventory of office supplies reveals $1,450 in office supplies on hand.

   d. The truck is depreciated straight-line with an estimated salvage value of $1,000 and an estimated useful life of five years.

   e. On November 1, 19X5, a $2,000 90-day note with 9% interest was made payable to Fulton Bank.

8. Next, complete the Adjusted Trial Balance columns on the worksheet below.

9. After completing the Adjusted Trial Balance columns, complete the Income Statement and Balance Sheet columns in the worksheet below.

Environmental Testing Services
Worksheet
for the year ended December 31 ,19X5

Account Name	Trial Balance Debit	Trial Balance Credit	Adjustments Debit	Adjustments Credit	Adjusted Trial Balance Debit	Adjusted Trial Balance Credit	Income Statement Debit	Income Statement Credit	Balance Sheet Debit	Balance Sheet Credit
Cash	1,500									
Accounts Receivable	320									
Prepaid Insurance	1,800									
Prepaid Rent	480									
Office Supplies	2,200									
Truck	19,000									
Accumulated Depreciation — Truck		3,600								
Accounts Payable		600								
Michelle Martin, Capital		17,100								
Michelle Martin, Withdrawal	2,600									
Testing Service Revenue		7,500								
Telephone Expense	900									
	28,800	28,800								
Insurance Expense										
Rent Expense										
Office Supplies Expense										
Depreciation Expense — Truck										
Interest Expense										
Interest Payable										
Net Income										

10. Which of the following is true about the preparation of financial statements?

    a. The total of the Balance Sheet debit column from the worksheet is equal to Total Assets on the formal Balance Sheet.

    b. The financial statements are prepared after the closing entries are completed.

    c. Formal financial statements are not required if a ten-column worksheet is prepared.

    d. Formal financial statements are prepared after the worksheet is completed.

11. After completing the worksheet for Environmental Testing Services, prepare formal financial statements for the year ended December 31, 19X5: Income Statement, Statement of Owner's Equity, and Balance Sheet

12. Which one of the following statements best describes the purposes of closing entries?

    a. to bring to zero the balances of the temporary or nominal accounts

    b. to update the Capital account to reflect the result of Revenue, Expense, and Withdrawal activity

    c. to bring to zero the balances of the real accounts

    d. Both (a) and (b) are correct

13. Which one of the following accounts would not be among those closed during the closing entry process?

    a. Michelle, Withdrawals

    b. Income Summary

    c. Accumulated Depreciation — Truck

    d. Depreciation Expense — Truck

14. Which of the following is a true statement concerning Income Summary?

    a. Income Summary is reported on the Income Statement.

    b. A debit balance in the account Income Summary indicates a net profit.

    c. The account Income Summary is closed to Owner's Capital during the closing entry process.

    d. All of the above are true.

15. From the completed worksheet for Environmental Testing Services, prepare the four closing journal entries.

16. Which of the following accounts would appear on the post-closing trial balance?

    a. Michelle Martin, Withdrawal

    b. Testing Fees, Revenue

    c. Accumulated Depreciation — Equipment

    d. Depreciation Expense — Equipment

17. What is a unique characteristic of the post-closing trial balance? Explain.

18. Prepare a post-closing trial balance for Environmental Testing Service.

19. Reversing entries:

    a. are optional.

    b. make the work of the bookkeeper easier.

    c. are appropriate for accrual-type adjusting entries only.

    d. All the above are true.

20. From the completed worksheet for Environmental Testing Services, prepare optional reversing entries.

Check Yourself

1. 5, 4, 1, 3, 2 (**Reviewing the steps in the accounting cycle**)

2. a. The source documents must be analyzed and processed in order to provide data for a trial balance, the first step in a worksheet. (**The 10-column worksheet**)

3. c. The ending balance of Michelle Martin, Capital, first appears on the formal financial statement, the Statement of Owner's Equity. It is also the balance that results upon completion of the closing entries. (a), (b), and (d) all appear on the ten-column worksheet. (**The 10-column worksheet**)

4. c. The income statement and balance-sheet columns are out of balance at the first footing. For the income statement columns, if the credit column is greater than the debit column, than the revenues are greater than the expenses. For the balance-sheet columns, if the debit column is greater than the credit column, than the inflow of assets is greater than the claim on those assets by outside creditors. Not (a) or (b) because the trial balance columns and the adjustments columns are in balance. (**The 10-column worksheet**)

5. d. If a loss occurs, expenses (the debit side of the Income Statement columns) exceed revenues; since a loss reduces owner's capital, it must appear on the debit side of the balance sheet columns. (**The 10-column worksheet**)

6. 3, 5, 1, 2, 4 (**The 10-column worksheet**)

7.

Environmental Testing Services **Worksheet** **for the year ended December 31 ,19X5**											
Account Name	Trial Balance		Adjustments		Adjusted Trial Balance		Income Statement		Balance Sheet		
	Debit	Credit	Debit	Credit	Debit	Credit	Debit	Credit	Debit	Credit	
Cash	1,500										
Accounts Receivable	320										
Prepaid Insurance	1,800			a) 1,200							
Prepaid Rent	480			b) 480							
Office Supplies	2,200			c) 750							
Truck	19,000										
Accumulated Depreciation — Truck		3,600		d) 3,600							
Accounts Payable		600									
Michelle Martin, Capital		17,100									
Michelle Martin, Withdrawal	2,600										
Testing Service Revenue		7,500									
Telephone Expense	900										
	28,800	28,800									
Insurance Expense			a) 1,200								
Rent Expense			b) 480								
Office Supplies Expense			c) 750								
Depreciation Expense — Truck			d) 3,600								
Interest Expense			e) 30								
Interest Payable				e) 30							
			6,060	6,060							
Net Income											

(The 10-column worksheet)

8.

	Environmental Testing Services Worksheet for the year ended December 31 ,19X5									
	Trial Balance		Adjustments		Adjusted Trial Balance		Income Statement		Balance Sheet	
Account Name	Debit	Credit	Debit	Credit	Debit	Credit	Debit	Credit	Debit	Credit
Cash	1,500				1,500					
Accounts Receivable	320				320					
Prepaid Insurance	1,800			a) 1,200	600					
Prepaid Rent	480			b) 480	—0—					
Office Supplies	2,200			c) 750	1,450					
Truck	19,000				19,000					
Accumulated Depreciation — Truck		3,600		d) 3,600		7,200				
Accounts Payable		600				600				
Michelle Martin, Capital		17,100				17,100				
Michelle Martin, Withdrawal	2,600				2,600					
Testing Service Revenue		7,500				7,500				
Telephone Expense	900				900					
	28,800	28,800								
Insurance Expense			a) 1,200		1,200					
Rent Expense			b) 480		480					
Office Supplies Expense			c) 750		750					
Depreciation Expense — Truck			d) 3,600		3,600					
Interest Expense			e) 30		30					
Interest Payable				e) 30		30				
			6,060	6,060	32,430	32,430				
Net Income										

(The 10-column worksheet)

9.

	Environmental Testing Services worksheet for the year ended December 31 ,19X5									
Account Name	Trial Balance		Adjustments		Adjusted Trial Balance		Income Statement		Balance Sheet	
	Debit	Credit	Debit	Credit	Debit	Credit	Debit	Credit	Debit	Credit
Cash	1,500				1,500				1,500	
Accounts Receivable	320				320				320	
Prepaid Insurance	1,800			a) 1,200	600				600	
Prepaid Rent	480			b) 480	—0—				—0—	
Office Supplies	2,200			c) 750	1,450				1,450	
Truck	19,000				19,000				19,000	
Accumulated Depreciation — Truck		3,600		d) 3,600		7,200				7,200
Accounts Payable		600				600				600
Michelle Martin, Capital		17,100				17,100				17,100
Michelle Martin, Withdrawal	2,600				2,600				2,600	
Testing Service Revenue		7,500				7,500		7,500		
Telephone Expense	900				900		900			
	28,800	28,800								
Insurance Expense			a) 1,200		1,200		1,200			
Rent Expense			b) 480		480		480			
Office Supplies Expense			c) 750		750		750			
Depreciation Expense — Truck			d) 3,600		3,600		3,600			
Interest Expense			e) 30		30		30			
Interest Payable				e) 30		30				30
			6,060	6,060	32,430	32,430	6,960	7,500	25,470	24,930
Net Income							540			540
							7,500	7,500	25,470	25,470

(The 10-column worksheet)

10. d. The formal financial statements are prepared following completion of the worksheet. Not (a) because the worksheet column does not include the subtraction for Accumulated Depreciation and it does include the Withdrawal amount. Not (b) because the closing entries are prepared only after the financial statements have been completed. Not (c) because the worksheet is not released outside the company; the formal financial statements convey information to decision makers in a more usable format. (**Preparing the financial statements**)

11.

Environmental Testing Services
Income Statement
for the year ended December 31 ,19X5

Testing Service Revenue		$7,500
Expenses		
Depreciation Expense — Truck	$3,600	
Insurance Expense	1,200	
Telephone Expense	900	
Office Supplies Expense	750	
Rent Expense	480	
Interest Expense	<u>30</u>	
Total Expenses		<u>6,960</u>
Net Income		<u>$540</u>

Environmental Testing Services
Statement of Owner's Equity
for the year ended December 31 ,19X5

Michelle Martin Capital, January 1, 19X5	$17,100
Add: Net Income	<u>540</u>
Subtotal	$17,640
Less: Michelle Martin, Withdrawals	<u>2,600</u>

11. (*continued*)

Michelle Martin Capital, Dec. 31, 19X5 $15,040

Environmental Testing Services
Balance Sheet
December 31 ,19X5

Assets			Liabilities	
Cash		$1,500	Accounts Payable	$600
Accounts Receivable		320	Interest Payable	30
Prepaid Insurance		600	Total liabilities	$630
Office Supplies		1,450		
Truck	19,000		Owner's Equity	
Less: Accumulated Depreciation — Truck	7,200	11,800	Michelle Martin, Capital	15,040

(Preparing the financial statements)

12. d. Not (c) because real accounts, i.e., Balance Sheet accounts, carry forward from one period to the next; they do not reach a zero balance. **(Preparing the financial statements)**

13. c. Accumulated Depreciation is a Balance Sheet account, a contra account to a depreciable asset account; it does not reach a zero balance until the end of the asset's life. **(Preparing the financial statements)**

14. c. One purpose of closing entries is to transfer the amount of net income to the Owner's Capital account. Not (a) because Income Summary is not reported on any financial statement; it is closed to Owner's Capital during the closing entry process. Not (b) because a credit balance in Income Summary indicates a net profit. **(Preparing the financial statements)**

15.

		Debit	Credit
1)	Testing Services Revenue	7,500	
	Income Summary		7,500
2)	Income Summary	6,960	
	Telephone Expense		900
	Insurance Expense		1,200
	Rent Expense		480
	Office Supplies Expense		750
	Depreciation Expense — Truck		3,600
	Interest Expense		30
3)	Income Summary	540	
	Michelle Martin, Capital		540
4)	Michelle Martin, Capital	2,600	
	Michelle Martin, Withdrawal		2,600

(Closing entries)

16. c. The post-closing trial balance contains only balance sheet accounts. Accumulated Depreciation — Equipment is a contra account to the asset account Equipment appearing on the Balance Sheet. Not (a), (b), or (d) because they are temporary or nominal accounts. **(Closing entries)**

17. The post-closing trial balance contains only balance sheet accounts; all the temporary accounts, i.e. those on the income statement and the withdrawal account, were brought to a zero balance during the closing entry process. **(Post-closing trial balance)**

18.

Environmental Testing Services
Post-closing Trial Balance
December 31, 19X5

	Debit	Credit
Cash	$1,500	
Accounts Receivable	320	
Prepaid Insurance	600	
Office Supplies	1,450	
Truck	19,000	
Accumulated Depreciation — Truck		$7,200
Accounts Payable		600
Interest Payable		30
Michelle Martin, Capital		15,040
	$22,870	$22,870

(Post-closing trial balance)

19. d. Reversing entries are not a requirement; they do eliminate the need for analysis of the related entry during the following period; they are used only for accrual type adjustments for which a cash transaction follows. **(Reversing entries)**

20.

	DR	CR
Interest Payable	30	
Interest Expense		30

(Reversing entries)

Grade Yourself

Circle the numbers of the questions you missed, then fill in the total incorrect for each topic. If you answered more than three questions incorrectly, you need to focus on that topic. (If a topic has less than three questions and you had at least one wrong, we suggest you study that topic also. Read your textbook, a review book, or ask your teacher for help.)

Subject: Completing the Accounting Cycle

Topic	Question Numbers	Number Incorrect
The 10-column worksheet	1, 2, 3, 4, 5, 6, 7, 8, 9	
Preparing the financial statements	10, 11, 12, 13, 14	
Closing entries	15, 16	
Post-closing trial balance	17, 18	
Reversing entries	19, 20	

Accounting for Merchandising Companies

5

Brief Yourself

In this chapter we focus on the merchandising company. We examine its characteristics, its journal entries, its computations, and its financial reporting.

A merchandising company makes money by selling a product. A merchandising company does not manufacture a product; instead, it buys a product from a manufacturer or from another merchandiser. So, in some transactions a merchandising company is a seller, and in others, it is a buyer. This contrast is an important one to note when analyzing journal entries.

The income statement of a merchandising company must report sales revenue and cost of the product sold separate from routine operating expenses. It also must report cash discounts and returns and allowances for both sales and purchases. Reporting freight costs is an added consideration of a merchandising company. Preparation of such an income statement requires additional levels of information not found in the income statement of a service company (as discussed in chapters 1–4).

A service company's income statement consists of three elements:

- revenues
- expenses
- net income.

A merchandising company's income statement contains five elements:

- revenues from sales
- cost of goods sold
- gross margin
- operating expenses
- net income

The matching rule, when applied to a merchandising company, dictates that costs necessary to generate revenues of the current period should be deducted from those revenues to arrive at net income of the same period. Also, costs that have future benefits should be carried on the balance sheet as assets, because they represent available resources. The accounting treatment for the cost of merchandise inventory is handled accordingly. If the inventory has been sold, then it generated the revenues of the current period and should be deducted from, or *matched* with, those revenues. Furthermore, once sold, that inventory has no future benefit to justify its asset status.

In reviewing journal entries, begin with the sales transaction. If payment is received immediately upon completion of a sale, we refer to it as a cash sale. If we bill the customer and expect to receive payment in the future, we call it a credit sale. Another term used to describe a credit sale is a sale made *on account*. Most of the examples you will encounter will be sales on account.

Review these journal entries:

Cash sales:

Cash	xx
Sales Revenue	xx

Credit sales:

Accounts Receivable xx	
Sales Revenue	xx

If a customer returns merchandise with your authorization, normally you would send the customer a *credit memo*. The accounting also must show that the amount the customer owes has been reduced. Sales Returns must be recorded in a separate account instead of making a direct reduction from the Sales Revenue account. Sales Returns and Allowances are a contra-account to Sales Revenue. By using a contra-account, Sales Revenue is reduced indirectly and a record of the returns is maintained. Since Sales Revenue is a credit balance account, the contra-account must be a debit balance account. The journal entry for a customer's return is:

Sales returns & allowances xx	
Accounts Receivable	xx

When a customer sends payment for the merchandise as a result of a credit sale, you must increase Cash and reduce Accounts Receivable:

Cash xx	
Accounts Receivable	xx

Some sellers offer the customer an opportunity to deduct a small percentage of the invoice at the time of payment. They do this to motivate the customer to pay quickly, usually within ten days. This reduction from the invoice total is called a *cash discount*. On an invoice, the cash discount may be identified by a notation similar to *Terms: 2/10, n/30*. From the seller's point of view, this cash discount is called a *Sales Discount*.

Hint: Do not confuse a *sales discount* with a *trade discount*; a trade discount is a reduction of the catalog list price. A trade discount is given for some reason other than the timing of the payment of the invoice, such as for a special promotion. A trade discount is not recorded.

If the timing of the customer's payment meets the seller's terms as stated on the invoice, then the journal entry is recorded as follows:

Cash	xx	
Sales Discounts	xx	
Accounts Receivable		xx

The Sales Discounts account is also a contra-account to the Sales Revenue account. Along with the Sales Returns and Allowances, it is deducted from the (Gross) Sales on the Income statement to arrive at the amount of Net Sales. In the Ledger, Sales Revenue is a credit balance account, whereas the two contra-accounts are debit balance accounts.

The *Merchandise Inventory*, or "the goods," is the product the company is in business to sell. We do not include the sale of the company's own office equipment, for instance, in inventory transactions.

When reviewing purchase transactions, keep in mind that there are two inventory systems to determine the amount of Cost of Goods Sold: the *periodic* inventory system and the *perpetual* inventory system. The periodic system is the one used in this chapter.

The periodic inventory system does not update the inventory balance during a period. If you look at the inventory account at any time during the period, it will contain the old beginning balance. The cause of that arises because events that lead to changes in inventory levels, such as additional purchases, sales, and returns, are recorded in accounts other than the inventory account. To arrive at the correct balance in inventory at the end of the period, the accountant must use one of two techniques: the *adjusting* entry method, or the *closing* entry method. These distinct techniques carry through from the worksheet to the closing entries.

The periodic inventory system requires a physical count of inventory at the end of a period. To calculate *Cost of Goods Sold,* the result of the physical count of ending inventory is deducted from the amount of *goods available* during the period. *Cost of Goods Sold only includes what was actually sold.* You will observe this calculation whenever you review a detailed Cost of Goods Sold section of an income statement.

The perpetual inventory method keeps an ongoing current balance in the inventory account by increasing the account directly whenever purchases are made and reducing the inventory account directly whenever goods are sold or returned. In this system, Cost of Goods Sold is an actual account in the ledger, not just a subtotal on the income statement.

The computation for Cost of Goods Sold is easier when divided into two steps. First, compute *Net Purchases* as follows:

	(Gross) purchases
−	Purchase discounts
−	<u>Purchase returns and allowances</u>
=	Subtotal
+	<u>Freight in</u>
=	Net purchases

To complete the Cost of Goods Sold computation, proceed as follows:

	Beginning inventory (at cost)
+	<u>Net purchases (see above)</u>
=	Goods available for sale (at cost)
−	<u>Ending inventory (at cost)</u>
=	<u>Cost of Goods Sold</u>

Two methods exist to record purchase transactions under the periodic system. One is the *gross* purchases method, the other the *net purchases* method. In each case, we assume that the merchandise has been purchased on credit.

The *gross* method records the purchase at the full amount appearing on the invoice. The purchase discount is recorded subsequently at the time payment is made. The initial journal entry you need to know is:

Purchases	xx	
Accounts Payable		xx

If your vendor authorizes you to return merchandise, your records should reflect that your liability to that vendor has been reduced. You also need to keep track of the return. It's best to set up a contra-account to Purchases, instead of directly reducing Purchases. Since Purchases is a debit balance account, the contra-account has to be a credit balance. The journal entry to record a purchase return appears as follows:

Accounts Payable	xx	
Purchase Returns & Allowances		xx

When sending payment for a purchase made on credit, the buyer must decrease the liability and decrease cash.

Accounts Payable	xx	
Cash		xx

If your payment is taking advantage of a cash discount a merchant offered you for quick payment, you are allowed to deduct a percentage, usually 2%, from the invoice total. Then your entry appears as follows:

Accounts Payable	xx	
Cash		xx
Purchase Discounts		xx

The Purchase Discount account is also a contra-account to Purchases and has a credit balance.

When recording a purchase using the net purchases method, the accounts used in the initial transaction are identical to the gross purchases method. The amount recorded is different, however, since the discount is deducted at the very beginning from the gross price.

When payment is made within the discount period, the journal entry recorded is:

Accounts Payable	xx	
Cash		xx

If payment is made after the discount period has expired, a Discounts Lost account is used. The journal entry recorded is:

Accounts Payable	xx	
Discounts Lost	xx	
Cash		xx

This technique is referred to as *Management by Exception*, because attention is drawn to the amount of the discounts lost reported as an operating expense. The advantage of the net purchases method is that a greater incentive exists to avoid missing the discount. Some accountants prefer the gross purchases method, however, because the potential exists under the net purchases method to understate liabilities.

Whether using the gross or the net method to record purchases, the accountant must consider the cost of freight transactions. *FO Shipping Point* and *FOB Destination* are terms that really pertain to the issue of when title of the goods transfers from the seller to the buyer. The distinction has an accounting significance, too. When the terms of the sale indicate:

FO Shipping Point, use the account Freight In, a component of Net Purchases and therefore reported in the Cost of Goods Sold section of the Income Statement. Hint: The buyer usually pays the freight.

The title on the goods transfers from the seller to the buyer when the goods leave the seller's loading dock. So while the goods are in transit, they are the inventory of the buyer.

FOB Destination, use the account Freight Out, a selling expense, and therefore reported in the operating expenses section of the Income Statement. Hint: The seller usually pays the freight.

The title transfers when the goods arrive at the buyer's destination. So while the goods are in transit, they are the inventory of the seller.

A special case that needs further explanation is FOB Shipping Point.

Purchases	xx	
Freight In	xx	
Accounts Payable		xx

In cases such as this, the cash discount is calculated on the Purchases amount only, not on the Freight In.

Test Yourself

1. Which of the following is an example of a merchandising company?

   a. Carmen Estrada Accounting Services

   b. Chip's Dependable Lawn Care

   c. Tortoise Book Store

   d. Peaches Moving Company

2. A deduction from a list price in a catalog is referred to as a:

   a. sales discount.

   b. trade discount.

   c. sales deduction.

   d. purchase deduction.

3. All of the following are accounts that may be entered in the journal *except*.

   a. sales discounts.

   b. sales returns and allowances.

   c. purchase discounts.

   d. trade discounts.

4. If a customer makes payment within the discount period, the journal entry for the merchandiser would include a:

   a. credit to Sales Discounts.

   b. credit to Purchase Discounts.

   c. debit to Sales.

   d. debit to Sales Discounts.

5. The Saint Paul Saints Souvenir Store engaged in the following sales transactions during the month of September 19X5. Record each transaction in general journal form. The Saint Paul Saints Souvenir Store grants terms of *2/10, n/30, FOB Shipping Point*, on all of its credit sales.

   Sept 2   Cash receipts for merchandise sold to patrons totaled $475.

   5   Credit sales for $2,200 in merchandise was shipped to Szabo Sporting Goods, a local distributor.

   9   A credit memo of $200 was issued to Szabo for merchandise returned from the Sept. 5 transaction.

   12   Sales for $3,000 in merchandise was shipped to Loring Specialty Stores, a local distributor, on account.

   15   Collected payment in full from Szabo for the September 5 sale.

   30   Collected payment in full from Loring for the Sept. 12 sale.

6. A perpetual inventory system would be most appropriate for which of the following companies?

   a. an exclusive designer clothing boutique

   b. a feed store in Kansas

   c. a discount shoe store

   d. a large discount drugstore

7. Szabo Sporting Goods entered into the following purchase transactions during the month of Sept. 19X5. Szabo Sporting Goods records its purchases using the gross purchase method and the periodic inventory system.

   Sept 5   Purchased $2,200 merchandise on credit, *terms 2/10, n/30, FOB Shipping Point*, from the Saint Paul Saints Souvenir Store.

   8   Paid $40 shipping costs to Gray Dog Shipping Company for the Sept. 5 purchase.

   9   Received a $200 credit memo from the Saint Paul Saints Souvenir Store for a segment of the merchandise purchased Sept. 5.

   11   Purchased $1,500 merchandise on credit from Torrence, Inc., for athletic shoes, terms *2/10, n/30, FOB Destination*.

   15   Sent payment in full to the Saint Paul Saints Souvenir Store for the Sept. 5 purchase.

17   Purchased merchandise on credit from Inman Manufacturing Company, terms *2/10, n/30, FOB Shipping Point, Freight Prepaid*. The amount of the invoice was $5,125, which included $125 freight and $5,000 merchandise.

19   Purchased store supplies, cash and carry, writing a check for $25.

27   Sent payment in full to Inman Manufacturing Company for the Sept. 17 purchase.

29   Sent payment in full to Torrence, Inc. for the Sept. 11 purchase.

8.   Loring Specialty Stores entered into the following purchase transactions during the month of September 19X5. Loring Specialty Stores records its purchases using the *net purchases method and the periodic inventory system*. Record each transaction in general journal form.

Sept 1   Purchased merchandise for $800 from Peachtree Olympic Supplies, terms *2/10, n/30, FOB Shipping Point*.

3   Received a credit memo of $50 from Peachtree Olympic Supplies for returned merchandise of Sept. 1 purchase.

5   Purchased $400 merchandise from Precision, Inc., on credit, terms *2/10, n/30, FOB Destination*.

9   Received a credit memo of $100 from Precision, Inc., for returned merchandise of Sept. 5 purchase.

10   Made full payment to Peachtree Olympic Supplies.

12   Purchased merchandise for $3,000 from Saint Paul Saints Souvenir Store, terms *2/10, n/30, FOB Shipping Point*.

29   Made full payment to Precision, Inc.

30   Paid Saint Paul Saints Souvenir Store in full for purchase of Sept. 12.

9.   The Saint Paul Saints Souvenir Store, which has a December 31 year-end, entered into the following transactions. Which one, if any, should be recorded in January?

a. Merchandise purchased FOB destination was shipped from the supplier on Dec. 20 and arrived Jan. 2.

b. Merchandise purchased FOB shipping point was shipped from the supplier on Dec. 21 and arrived Jan. 4.

c. Merchandise sold FOB shipping point was shipped on Dec. 29 and arrived at the Minnesota Mall Store Jan. 3.

d. All of the above should be recorded in January.

10.   The Saint Paul Saints Souvenir Store, which has a Dec. 31 year end, entered into the following transactions. Which units of merchandise, if any, should be included in their Dec. 31, 19X4, year-end inventory?

a. Merchandise purchased, terms FOB destination, was shipped from the supplier on Dec. 20 and arrived at the souvenir shop Jan. 2.

b. Merchandise purchased, terms FOB shipping point, was shipped from the supplier on Dec. 21 and arrived at the souvenir shop Jan. 4.

c. Merchandise sold as a courtesy to another vendor, The Minnesota Mall Store, terms FOB shipping point, was shipped by the souvenir shop on Dec. 29 and arrived at the mall store Jan. 3.

d. All of the above merchandise should be included in Dec. 31, 1994, year-end inventory.

11.   Where, among the last four columns of the ten-column worksheet for Saint Paul Saints Souvenir Store, would the Purchase Returns and Allowances appear?

a. on the Balance Sheet debit column

b. on the Balance Sheet credit column

c. on the Income Statement debit column

d. on the Income Statement credit column

12. All of the following are included in the calculation of net purchases *except*:

    a. purchases.

    b. freight-out.

    c. purchase discounts.

    d. purchase returns and allowances.

13. Which of the following is included in cost of goods available for sale but not included in cost of goods sold?

    a. beginning inventory

    b. purchases

    c. ending inventory

    d. freight-in

14. Compute the dollar amount of each missing item. Treat each column as a separate problem set.

	1	2	3	4
Sales	$300,000	(d)	$450,000	$750,000
Beginning Inventory	(a)	$20,000	40,000	75,000
Net Purchases	160,000	(e)	330,000	(i)
Ending Inventory	15,000	32,000	(f)	100,000
Cost of Goods Sold	(b)	214,000	(g)	(j)
Gross Margin	60,000	118,000	90,000	(k)
Operating Expenses	(c)	82,000	(h)	250,000
Net Income (Loss)	$35,000	$36,000	$(5,000)	$65,000

Check Yourself

1. c. Books are the merchandise sold. Accounting services (a), lawn care (b), and moving (d) are examples of companies that earn revenues from services rendered. (**Characteristics of a merchandising company**)

2. b. A trade discount is a deduction from a catalog list price and is offered in instances of large volume sales and/or special promotions of products. A sales discount (a) is an example of a cash discount offered to encourage quick payment by a customer. (**Discounts for merchandising companies**)

3. d. A trade discount is deducted from the list price and is not recognized in the accounting records. If a trade discount has been extended, the invoice total is the catalog list price less the trade discount. Sales discounts (a), sales returns and allowances (b), and purchase discounts are all examples of contra accounts which are recognized in journal entries. (**Discounts for merchandising companies**)

4. d. The merchandiser is the seller. Sales Discounts, a contra account to Sales, has a normal debit balance, the opposite to the credit balance of the Sales account. Therefore not (a) or (c). A credit to Purchase Discounts is correct on the buyer's books. (**Discounts for merchandising companies**)

5.

Sept.	2	Cash	475	
		Sales		475
	5	Accounts Receivable	2,200	
		Sales		2,200
	9	Sales Returns and Allowances	200	
		Accounts Receivable		200
	12	Accounts Receivable	3,000	
		Sales		3,000
	15	Cash	1,960	
		Sales Discounts	40*	
		Accounts Receivable		2,000
	30	Cash	3,000	
		Accounts Receivable		3,000

*[2% ($2,000–$200): no discount is taken on the merchandise returned.]
(**Sales transactions**)

6. a. It is more important for a merchant of high-priced inventory to maintain a close control of inventory.
    (Perpetual and periodic inventory systems)

7. Sept.

Sept.	5	Purchases	2,200	
		Accounts Payable		2,200
	8	Freight-in	40	
		Cash		40
	9	Accounts Payable	200	
		Purchase Returns and Allowances		200
	11	Purchases	1,500	
		Accounts Payable		1,500
	15	Accounts Payable	2,000	
		Purchase Discounts		40*
		Cash		1,960
	17	Purchases	5,000	
		Freight-in	125	
		Accounts Payable		5,125
	19	Store Supplies	25	
		Cash		25
	27	Accounts Payable	5,125	
		Purchase Discounts		100**
		Cash		5,025
	29	Accounts Payable	1,500	
		Cash		1,500

*[2%($2,200-$200): no discount is taken on the merchandise returned]

**[2%($5,000): no discount is taken on the freight]

(Purchase transactions — gross purchase method)

8.

Sept.	1	Purchases	784	
		Accounts Payable		784
	3	Accounts Payable	49	
		Purchase Returns and Allowances		49
	5	Purchases	392	
		Accounts Payable		392
	9	Accounts Payable	98	
		Purchase Returns and Allowances		98
	10	Accounts Payable	735	
		Cash		735
	12	Purchases	2,940	
		Accounts Payable		2,940
	29	Accounts Payable	294	
		Cash		294
	30	Accounts Payable	2,940	
		Purchase Discounts Lost	60	
		Cash		3,000

Hint: The Net Purchases method assumes all payments will be made within the discount period. The cost of merchandise is recorded at the time of purchase with the discount deducted from the gross purchase amount; no purchase discount is recorded. If payment is made after the discount period has expired, the *Purchase Discounts Lost* or *Discounts Lost* account is used to record the additional cost. (**Purchase transactions — net purchase method**)

9. a. According to the terms FOB destination, title transfers on merchandise at the time the merchandise arrives at the destination. This becomes a Jan. 2 transaction, the day the merchandise arrives. (b) and (c) are December transactions. (**Accounting for freight transactions**)

10. b. According to the terms FOB shipping point, title transfers on goods when they are shipped. So the title of the merchandise passes to the souvenir shop on Dec. 21, 19X4, although they remain in transit at year end. Not (a) because title doesn't transfer to the souvenir shop until Jan. 2 upon arrival. Not (c) because title transfers to the Minnesota Mall Store on December 29, the day they were shipped. (**Accounting for freight transactions**)

11. d. Purchase Returns and Allowances is a contra-account to the Income Statement account Purchases. Since Purchases, a cost, has a debit balance, its contra-account must have the opposite balance, a credit. Not (a), (b), or (c). (**Worksheet for a merchandising company**)

12. b. Freight-out is a selling expense, reported in the operating expense section of the income statement. Purchases (a), purchase discounts (c), and purchase returns and allowances (d) are included in net purchases. (**Income statement for a merchandising company**)

13. c. Ending inventory is deducted from cost of goods available for sale to arrive at cost of goods sold. Beginning inventory, purchases, and freight-in are all included in cost of goods sold. (**Income statement for a merchandising company**)

14.

	1	2	3	4
Sales	$300,000	332,000	$450,000	$750,000
Beginning Inventory	95,000	$20,000	40,000	75,000
Net Purchases	160,000	226,000	330,000	460,000
Ending Inventory	15,000	32,000	10,000	100,000
Cost of Goods Sold	240,000	214,000	360,000	435,000
Gross Margin	60,000	118,000	90,000	315,000
Operating Expenses	25,000	82,000	95,000	250,000
Net Income (Loss)	$35,000	$36,000	$(5,000)	$65,000

#1

Beginning Inventory	a) $95,000	Sales	$300,000
+ Net Purchases	+ 160,000	– Cost of Goods Sold	–240,000
= Cost of Goods Available for Sales	= 255,000	= Gross Margin	= 60,000
– Ending Inventory	–15,000	– Operating Expenses	c) 25,000
= Cost of Goods Sold	b) $240,000	= Net Income (Loss)	$35,000

14. (*continued*)

#2

Beginning Inventory	$20,000	Sales	d) $332,000
+ Net Purchases	e) 226,000	– Cost of Goods Sold	– 214,000
= Cost of Goods Available for Sales	$246,000	= Gross Margin	= $118,000
– Ending Inventory	– 32,000	– Operating Expenses	– 82,000
= Cost of Goods Sold	$214,000	= Net Income (Loss)	$36,000

#3

Beginning Inventory	$40,000	Sales	$450,000
+ Net Purchases	+ 330,000	– Cost of Goods Sold	– g) 360,000
= Cost of Goods Available for Sales	= 370,000	= Gross Margin	= $90,000
– Ending Inventory	– f) 10,000	– Operating Expenses	– h) 95,000
= Cost of Goods Sold	g) $360,000	= Net Income (Loss)	= $(5,000)

#4

Beginning Inventory	$75,000	Sales	$750,000
+ Net Purchases	+ i) 460,000	– Cost of Goods Sold	– j) 435,000
= Cost of Goods Available for Sales	= $535,000	= Gross Margin	k) $315,000
– Ending Inventory	– 100,000	– Operating Expenses	– 250,000
= Cost of Goods Sold	j) $435,000	= Net Income (Loss)	= $65,000

(Income statement for a merchandising company)

Grade Yourself

Circle the numbers of the questions you missed, then fill in the total incorrect for each topic. If you answered more than three questions incorrectly, you need to focus on that topic. (If a topic has less than three questions and you had at least one wrong, we suggest you study that topic also. Read your textbook, a review book, or ask your teacher for help.)

Subject: Accounting for Merchandising Companies

Topic	Question Numbers	Number Incorrect
Characteristics of merchandising companies	1	
Discounts for merchandising companies	2, 3, 4	
Sales transactions	5	
Perpetual and periodic inventory systems	6	
Purchase transactions — gross purchase method	7	
Purchase transactions — net purchase method	8	
Accounting for freight transactions	9, 10	
Work sheet for a merchandising company	11	
Income statement for a merchandising company	12, 13, 14	

Internal Control and Control of Cash

6

Brief Yourself

In this chapter we review the characteristics of internal control and examine how, specifically, it is applied to a very important and highly vulnerable asset, that of *Cash*.

Internal control is a system that:

a) safeguards a company's *assets*.

b) checks the *accuracy* and *reliability* of a company's *accounting data*.

c) promotes a company's *operational efficiency*.

d) encourages *adherence* within a company to prescribed *managerial policies*.

Examples of control procedures are:

a) *authorization* for certain transactions.

b) *recording* of all *transactions*.

c) design and use of adequate *documents* and *records*.

d) *limited access* to assets.

e) periodic *independent verification* of records.

f) *separation of duties*.

g) sound *personnel procedures*.

The *bank reconciliation* is a key step in a company's *internal control system* because it explains the *difference* between the *cash balance* as reflected in the company's *accounting records* versus the *bank statement*.

The section of the bank reconciliation pertaining to the *balance per books* provides the data to perform the adjusting of journal entries. If these adjustments are not made, the *cash account* in the *general ledger* would fail to reflect the updated balance per the reconciliation.

Although it is the best method a company has available to control cash disbursements, writing checks is not always practical or possible. For those situations, establishing and maintaining an *imprest petty cash system* is the next best alternative. *Two journal entries* are needed to establish and maintain an *imprest petty cash system*.

1)   Petty Cash   xx
             Cash   xx
             (To *establish the fund*)

2)   Various expenses   xx
             Cash   xx
             (To *replenish the fund*)

The *Petty Cash Account* is an account in the general ledger. It is assigned a number in the chart of accounts as is any account in the general ledger. *Note: Generally, Petty Cash is debited just one time, when the fund is established, and never again.*

Another means companies use to control cash is the *voucher system*. It is an internal control measure that ensures that every company check written is supported by an approval from an authorized individual who is different from the check signer. A voucher system is an implementation of the rule of *separation of duties*.

The components of the voucher system are: 1) the *voucher register*; and 2) the *check register*.

Test Yourself

1.   Which of the following company strategies and/or procedures is not part of the internal control structure?

a. the market survey

b. the personnel policies

c. the accounting system

d. the internal review

2.   Which of the following situations violates the principle of separation of duties?

a. The company maintains a voucher system for all its cash expenditures.

b. The inventory stock clerk handles the inventory records.

c. A mail-room employee handles postal cash receipts.

d. The cashier does not have access to the tape locked inside the cash register that records each sale.

3. If a company issues a check for $235 but records it as $253, how should the $18 difference be handled on the bank reconciliation?

   a. added to the balance per the bank statement

   b. deducted from the balance per the bank statement

   c. added to the balance per the books

   d. deducted from the balance per the books

4. Which of the following reconciling items from the bank reconciliation would be followed with an adjusting entry?

   a. a bank error

   b. the outstanding checks

   c. a customer's NSF check

   d. a night deposit made on the last business day of the month

5. The reconciling items listed below pertain to Lewis Company for the month of November 19X5. Place an X in the appropriate column.

	Add to the bank balance	Deduct from the bank balance	Add to the book balance	Deduct from the book balance
Deposit in transit				
Collection made by bank from customer deposit				
Bank service charge				
Interest earned on checking balance				
A customer's NSF check				
Outstanding checks				
Bookkeeping error: understating a check				
Bank error: charge for check belonging to another company				
Bookkeeping error: overstating a deposit				

6. From the reconciling items provided, prepare a bank reconciliation for DEF Company as of September 30, 19X5.

   a. The ending cash balance per the bank statement was $16,275.73. The general ledger account Cash reflected a balance of $11,427.08 for the same date.

   b. A deposit of $2,610.47, the total of cash receipts for September 30, did not appear on the bank statement.

   c. Checks that had not cleared and were still outstanding as of September 30 totaled $1,968.40. They were check numbers 305, 308, and 311 for $1,000.00, $700.00, and $268.40, respectively.

   d. Upon comparing the canceled checks returned with the statement to the check register, it was discovered that a check actually written for $960.00 was recorded as $690.00. The check was a payment on Accounts Payable.

   e. Bank service charges for September amounted to $12.50.

   f. The bank collected $6,120.00 from a DEF customer on behalf of DEF Company. This was the result of a $6,000.00 note that had earned $120.00 in interest at the time of maturity.

   g. A check for $91.78 from a DEF customer, Jim Jenkins, was returned marked NSF (non-sufficient funds).

   h. By mistake the bank deducted $425.00 from DEF Company's balance the amount of a check written by another company with a similar account number.

   i. The bank statement reflected an additional $170.00 interest earned on the average daily balance of DEF Company's account.

7. From the completed bank reconciliation, prepare the adjusting journal entries.

8. Upon completion of the bank reconciliation and the journal entries, what amount for cash will appear on the DEF Company formal balance sheet dated September 30, 19X5?

9. After careful consideration, Environmental Testing Services established an *imprest* petty cash system to facilitate payment of small cash expenditures in instances when payment by check is either not possible or not practical. The measures taken to strengthen the verity of the system included: appointment of a trustworthy petty cash custodian, selection of a secure location for the petty cash, printing of pre-numbered petty cash vouchers, and the preparation of written procedures.

For each of the following transactions, prepare the necessary general journal entry:

March 1 A petty cash fund was established for $250.

31 Routine count of the petty cash fund revealed that $35 coins and currency remained in the petty cash safe. Examination of authorized March petty cash vouchers revealed reimbursements of $55 for employee parking and mileage, $45 for postage, $65 for supplies, and $50 for laundering uniforms.

April 30 Routine count of the petty cash fund revealed that $40 coins and currency remained in the petty cash safe. Examination of authorized April petty cash vouchers revealed reimbursements of $50 for employee parking and mileage, $30 for postage, $60 for supplies, and $65 for laundering uniforms.

10. GHI Company uses a voucher system to maintain good internal control over all cash disbursements. In January 19X6, GHI Company had the following transaction. Record the transactions in the appropriate registers provided.

   a. Prepared voucher no. 3150 to Southeastern Bell for telephone expense, $62.00.

   b. Issued check no. 415 for voucher no. 3150.

   c. Prepared voucher no. 3151, $450.00, to Aranyi Real Estate for January rent.

   d. Issued check no. 416 for voucher no. 3151.

   e. Prepared voucher no. 3152, $525.00, to Inman Office Supplies to be allocated to Office Supplies, $325.00, and to Store Supplies, $200.00.

   f. Prepared voucher no. 3153 to Presto Parts, $1,000, for merchandise, terms 2/10, n/30.

   g. Issued check no. 417 for voucher no. 3153, within the discount period.

   h. Prepared voucher no. 3154 for $238.00 to authorize replenishment of petty cash. Supporting petty cash vouchers consisted of $100 for Laundry Expense and $138 for Employee Travel Expense.

   i. Prepared voucher no. 3155 to transfer $5,000.00 to the payroll checking account for the January payroll to be paid on the first day of February.

   j. Issued check no. 418 to replenish petty cash per voucher no. 3154.

11. Assuming there were no outstanding unpaid vouchers at the end of the month of December 19X5, what is the total amount to be reported in the payables section of the Balance Sheet of GHI Company as of January 31, 19X6?

Check Yourself

1. a. **(Internal control)**

2. b. The individual with access to the asset should not have the record-keeping function for that asset. **(Internal control)**

3. c. **(Control of cash—bank reconciliation)**

4. c. **(Control of cash—bank reconciliation)**

5.

	Add to the bank balance	Deduct from the bank balance	Add to the book balance	Deduct from the book balance
Deposit in transit	X			
Collection made by bank from customer deposit			X	
Bank service charge				X
Interest earned on checking balance			X	
A customer's NSF check				X
Outstanding checks		X		
Bookkeeping error: understating a check				X
Bank error: charge for check belonging to another company	X			
Bookkeeping error: overstating a deposit				X

(Control of cash—bank reconciliation)

6.

DEF Company
Bank Reconciliation
for the month ended September 30, 19X5

Balance per the Bank				$16,275.73
Add:	Deposit in transit		$2,610.47	
	Bank error		425.00	3,035.47
				$19,311.20
Less:	Outstanding checks	#305	$1,000.00	
		#308	700.00	
		#311	268.40	
				1,968.40
Adjusted Bank Balance				$17,342.80
Balance per Books				$11,427.08
Add:	Note plus interest collected by bank		$6,120.00	
	Interest earned on average daily balance		170.00	6,290.00
				$17,717.08
Less:	Recording error on books		$270.00	
	Customer bounced check — Jim Jenkins		91.78	
	Bank service charge		12.50	374.28
Adjusted Book Balance				$17,342.80

(Control of cash—bank reconciliation)

7.

	DR	CR
Cash	6,290.00	
Note Receivable		6,000.00
Interest Income		290.00
Accounts Payable	270.00	
Accounts Receivable	91.78	
Bank Service Charge Expense	12.50	
Cash		374.28

Without the follow-up journal entries upon completion of the bank reconciliation, the cash balance in the general ledger reflects the unadjusted balance. The goal is to update the cash balance on the books from the new information provided by the bank reconciliation.

The company accountant has control only over adjustments to the company books. Only reconciling items affecting the book balance may be adjusted. Reconciling items pertaining to the bank balance usually are timing differences, as in the case of the deposit in transit and the outstanding checks. If the reconciling item is a bank error, then the bank is expected to correct the error once it is notified.

(Journal entries following a bank reconciliation)

8. $17,342.80

Cash		
Balance	11,427.08	
	6,290.00	374.28
Adjusted Balance	17,342.80	

(Cash balance to report on balance sheet)

9.

			DR	CR
March	1	Petty Cash	250	
		Cash		250
	31	Employee local travel expense	55	
		Postage expense	45	
		Supplies	65	
		Laundry expense	50	
		Cash		215

(The amount needed for replenishment is exactly equal to the total of the petty cash expenditures supported by vouchers.)

April	30	Employee local travel expense	50	
		Postage expense	30	
		Supplies	60	
		Laundry expense	65	
		Cash short/over	5	
		Cash		210

(The total of petty cash expenditures supported by vouchers is five dollars less than the amount needed for replenishment, indicating a shortage of $5.)

(Petty cash)

10.

			Payment		Credit	Debit				Tele-		
Date	Voucher Number	Payee		Date/ Check #	Vouchers Payable	Pur- chases	Office Supplies	Store Supplies	phone Expense		Other Accounts	Debit

GHI Company / Voucher Register

Date	Voucher Number	Payee		Date/Check #	Vouchers Payable	Pur-chases	Office Supplies	Store Supplies	Telephone Expense		Other Accounts	Debit
a	3150	Southeastern Bell	b	415	62.00				62.00			
c	3151	Aranyi Real Estate	d	416	450.00					c	Rent Expense	450.00
e	3152	Inman Office Supplies			525.00		325.00	200.00				
f	3153	Presto Parts	g	417	1,000.00	1,000.00						
h	3154	replenish petty cash	j	418	238.00					h	Laundry Expense Employee Travel Expense	100.00 138.00
i	3155	transfer to payroll checking			5,000.00					i	Wage Expense	5,000.00

GHI Company / Check Register

Check Number	Date	Payee	Voucher Number	Debit	Credits	
				Vouchers Payable	Purchase Discounts	Cash
415	b	Southeastern Bell	3150	62.00		62.00
416	d	Aranyi Real Estate	3151	450.00		450.00
417	g	Presto Parts	3153	1,000.00	20.00	980.00
418	j	Cash	3154	238.00		238.00

(The voucher system)

11. $5,525.00 (unpaid vouchers 3152 for $525.00, and 3155 for $5,000.00)   **(The voucher system)**

Grade Yourself

Circle the numbers of the questions you missed, then fill in the total incorrect for each topic. If you answered more than three questions incorrectly, you need to focus on that topic. (If a topic has less than three questions and you had at least one wrong, we suggest you study that topic also. Read your textbook, a review book, or ask your teacher for help.)

Subject: Internal Control and Control of Cash

Topic	Question Numbers	Number Incorrect
Internal control	1, 2	
Control of cash—bank reconciliation	3, 4, 5, 6	
Journal entries following a bank reconciliation	7	
Cash balance to report on balance sheet	8	
Petty cash	9	
The voucher system	10, 11	

Short-Term Liquid Assets

7

Brief Yourself

In this chapter we focus on accounting for *short-term liquid assets*. When using this term we are referring to *short-term investments* or *short-term marketable securities*, *accounts receivable*, and *short-term notes receivable*.

Short-term Investments

Companies purchase *short-term investments* when they possess idle cash. Short-term investments are classified on the balance sheet as a *current asset*. Short-term investments consist of *equity* securities and *debt* securities. *Equity* securities are investments in shares of stock, units of ownership, of companies. Equity securities yield earnings in the form of *dividend income*.

Debt securities are forms of credit extended to companies or governmental entities. Corporate bonds and U.S. Treasury bills are examples. Debt securities yield earnings in the form of *interest income*.

For both *equity securities* and *debt securities*, the *acquisition* is recorded as:

      Short-term Investments   xx
          Cash   xx

For *equity securities*, the *receipt of earnings* is recorded as follows:

      Cash   xx
          Dividend Income   xx

For *debt securities* such as U.S. Treasury Bills, *earnings* are recorded *at maturity*:

      Cash   xx
          Interest Income   xx
          Short-term Investments   xx

Equity securities can be sold for cash, usually at a gain or a loss. *If the cash received is greater than the original investment cost, a gain (a credit balance account) is recorded. If the cash received is less than the original investment cost, a loss (a debit balance account) is recorded.*

Accounts Receivable

When accounting for Accounts Receivable, care must be exercised to observe the tenets of the *matching rule*. The need arises even for companies that practice stringent policies concerning extensions of credit to customers. Whenever a sale has been made *on account*, a risk is incurred that potential nonpayment will result. So, although selling on credit usually reaps significant benefits, occasionally costs are incurred.

The *expense* resulting from a customer's default on a payment should be *matched* against the *revenue* earned in the period of that sale. This is an application of the *matching rule*. A company cannot know at the time it extends credit which customer will eventually default on its payment. Therefore, the loss must be *estimated* in order to be recorded in the same accounting period as the revenue.

The *Allowance for Uncollectible Accounts* is a *Contra-Asset* account to *Accounts Receivable*. It is reported on the *Balance Sheet*. In the general ledger, it is an account that stays open with an ongoing balance.

The *Uncollectible Accounts Expense* account is reported on the *Income Statement* as an *operating expense*. Its balance is closed to income summary each year.

Two approaches exist to adjust the balances in these accounts. One is the *percentage of net sales* method; the other is the *aging of accounts receivable* method.

The *percentage of net sales* method is the easier of the two methods to calculate. If management selects this method, it is focusing on the income statement. You will be given a percentage that the management has estimated as the amount of sales that will be uncollectible. Simply multiply that percentage times the amount of *net sales* for the period. The result of your computation equals the amount of uncollectible accounts expense you record, regardless of the existing balance in the allowance account. Remember, this number is an *estimate*.

The *aging of accounts receivable* method examines the age of the individual accounts in accounts receivable. This is done because experience has proven that a correlation exists between the age of an account and the probability that a default will occur. The important point when using the aging method is to force the adjustment to be an amount that will make the balance in the allowance for uncollectible accounts account equal to the result of the aging analysis. Unlike the percentage of net sales method, which emphasizes the income statement, the aging of accounts receivable method places an emphasis on the balance sheet.

Only one journal entry exists to *record uncollectible accounts expense*. The amount of the adjustment varies according to which method is chosen to *estimate*. The entry, prepared at *year-end* because it is an *adjusting entry*, appears as follows:

Uncollectible Accounts Expense	xx	
Allowance for Uncollectible Accounts		xx

A *write-off* of an account judged uncollectible can be made at *any time during the year*. Usc the *actual* amount of the customer's account balance as the amount of the write-off. The entry appears as follows:

Allowance for Uncollectible Accounts	xx	
Accounts Receivable		xx

If an account previously written off results in a subsequent collection, *two journal entries* must be prepared:

Accounts Receivable	xx	
Allowance for Uncollectible Accounts		xx
(to reinstate the account balance by *reversing the write-off entry*)		

Cash	xx	
Accounts Receivable		xx
(to record the *collection of cash* and the *reduction of Accounts Receivable*)		

Short-term Notes Receivable

A *promissory note* is a document received from another company, the *maker* of the note, which owes the company money. On the note, the maker indicates, in writing, the specified amount to be repaid and the repayment terms, including due date and interest rate. The company to which the money is owed is referred to as the *payee*. In the context of this chapter, *Short-Term Liquid Assets*, the focus is directed to the payee, who records the receipt of the note as *Notes Receivable*. Accounting for notes from the maker's position, as a liability, is presented in a later chapter.

When determining the *maturity date* of a note, one does not include the day the note is made. Day #1 begins the following day. The maturity date is then the 30th, 60th, or 90th day, etc., according to the terms of the note. Note that some months have 31 days, others only 30, with February containing only 28 days. These details will affect the due date of a note. You should know the number of days in each month without consulting a calendar.

The *maturity value* of a note is the sum of its face value and the interest to be earned from the note. To compute *interest income* on a note, use the following formula:

$$Face\ value\ (Principal) \times annual\ interest\ rate \times \frac{\#\ of\ days}{360}$$

The *bank's fee* upon discounting a note receivable is calculated as follows:

$$Maturity\ value \times bank\ discount\ rate \times \frac{\#\ of\ days\ reamining\ on\ the\ note}{360}$$

The cash proceeds is determined by subtracting the bank's fee from the maturity value.

The *interest income* (or expense) is calculated by subtracting the face value from the cash proceeds. If the amount is positive, then it is referred to as interest income. If it is negative (i.e., the cash received is less than the note itself), it is referred to as interest expense.

The entry to record the *receipt of a note* that is to satisfy an accounts receivable balance is:

Notes Receivable	xx	
Accounts Receivable		xx

Another possible explanation for the receipt of a note includes accepting a note immediately upon making a sale. In that case, the journal entry would appear as:

Notes Receivable	xx	
Sales Revenue		xx

or, simply lending an entity cash, which would be recorded as follows:

Notes Receivable	xx	
Cash		xx

The *collection of a note* takes place on the maturity date and includes the collection of the *interest income*, requiring a compound journal entry:

Cash	xx	
Notes Receivable		xx
Interest Income		xx

Accrual adjusting entries are prepared to record interest receivable and interest income at year-end, if the year-end occurs between the date the note is made and the maturity date. The journal entry to use is:

(Accrued) Interest Receivable	xx	
Interest Income		xx

 # Test Yourself

1. All of the following are short-term liquid assets *except*:

   a. accounts receivable.

   b. notes receivable due within 90 days.

   c. certificates of deposit.

   d. inventory.

2. Short-term marketable securities are presented on the balance sheet at:

   a. market value, no matter whether it has increased or decreased.

   b. cost or market, whichever is lower.

c. historical cost.

d. an average of the cost and the market.

3. JKL Company invested its idle cash in short-term investments of marketable securities and U.S. Treasury bills. JKL Company used one account called Short-Term Investments in its general ledger. Record the following transactions in general journal form.

a. Purchased for $146,000, U.S. Treasury bills that will mature in 120 days at $150,000.

b. Purchased 5,000 shares of South-Central Utility Company stock for $25 per share.

c. Purchased 8,000 shares of Forrest-Atlantic Paper Company stock for $40 per share.

d. The U.S. Treasury bills matured; cash was received for the invested amount plus the related income.

e. Purchased 3,000 shares of Abbot Entertainment Company stock for $22 per share.

f. Quarterly cash dividend checks were received from both South-Central Utility Company and Forrest-Atlantic Paper Company. The per-share amounts received from the companies were ten cents and fifteen cents, respectively.

g. Sold 3,000 shares of the South-Central Utility Company stock for $28 per share.

h. Sold all shares of the Forrest-Atlantic Paper Company stock for $37 per share.

4. Why is the direct charge-off method of handling bad debts considered unacceptable under generally accepted accounting principles?

a. It violates the conservatism convention.

b. It violates the consistency convention.

c. It violates the matching principle.

d. None of the above; the direct charge-off method is always acceptable.

5. MNO Company uses the percentage-of-sales method to estimate its Uncollectible Accounts Expense. On January 1, 19X5, its general ledger reflected balances for Accounts Receivable and Allowance for Uncollectible Accounts of $400,000 and $6,800, respectively. Credit sales during 19X5 totaled $500,000, collections on account totaled $490,000, and customer accounts written off totaled $6,500. It is estimated that 1 1/2% of credit sales are uncollectible. Based on this data:

a. prepare the 19X5 year-end adjusting journal entry to record uncollectible accounts expense, and;

b. provide the 19X5 year-end general ledger balances for Uncollectible Accounts Expense and the Allowance for Uncollectible Accounts.

6. From the data provided below:

a. complete the aging schedule, and;

b. compute the amount required balance for the allowance for uncollectible accounts.

Age of Account	Year-end Balance of Accounts Receivable	Percentage Uncollectible	Amount Required in Allowance Account
1–30 days	$22,000	1	
31–60 days	38,000	2	
61–90 days	18,000	10	
over 90 days	12,000	40	
	$90,000		

7. PQR Company uses the aging-of-accounts-receivable method to estimate its Uncollectible Accounts Expense. On January 1, 19X5, its general ledger reflected balances for Accounts Receivable and Allowance for Uncollectible Accounts of $400,000 and $6,800, respectively. Credit sales during 19X5 totaled $500,000, collections on account totaled $490,000, and customer accounts written off totaled $6,500. Based on the aging schedule prepared for Question 6:

   a. prepare the 19X5 year-end adjusting journal entry to record uncollectible accounts expense, and;

   b. provide the 19X5 year-end balances for Uncollectible Accounts Expense and the Allowance for Uncollectible Accounts.

8. PQR Company uses the aging-of-accounts-receivable method to estimate its Uncollectible Accounts Expense. On January 1, 19X5, its general ledger reflected balances for Accounts Receivable and Allowance for Uncollectible Accounts of $400,000 and $6,100, respectively. Credit sales during 19X5 totaled $500,000, collections on account totaled $490,000, and customer accounts written off totaled $6,500. Based on the aging schedule prepared for Question 6:

   a. prepare the 19X5 year-end adjusting journal entry to record uncollectible accounts expense, and;

   b. provide the 19X5 year-end balances for Uncollectible Accounts Expense and the Allowance for Uncollectible Accounts.

9. Prepare the journal entry to record the write-off of customers' accounts as mentioned in the above questions.

10. After $6,500 in customer accounts had been written off, PQR received a letter along with a check for $1,500 from a customer whose account for that amount had been included in the write-off. Record in general journal the reinstatement and recovery of the customer's balance.

11. A 90-day short-term note is issued on March 1. It is due on:

   a. May 29

   b. May 30

   c. May 31

   d. June 1

12. Thomas Company discounts a 90-day, 8%, $9,000 note at the bank 30 days after it was received. The bank charges a discount rate of 12%. On the day it records the cash proceeds, Thomas Company will also record:

   a. Interest expense, $3.60

   b. Interest income, $3.60

   c. Interest expense, $88.20

   d. Interest income, $88.20

13. Record in general journal form the following transactions of Mnemonic Company, pertaining to promissory notes.

   a. On October 1, Mnemonic Company sold merchandise with a selling price of $9,200 to Kellner Company, terms n/30.

   b. On October 31, Mnemonic Company receives from Kellner Company a $5,000, 9%, 60-day note, upon learning from Kellner Company that currently it can pay only $4,200 due to a cash flow problem.

   c. On December 31, Mnemonic Company receives payment in full from Kellner Company.

14. Record in general journal form the following transactions of Melter Company pertaining to promissory notes.

   a. Melter Company accepted a 90-day, 9% note from Lester Company on November 1, 19X1, as payment for a sale of merchandise of $8,000.

   b. Melter Company, which had a December 31 year-end, prepared adjusting entries and closing entries.

   c. On January 30, 19X2, Melter Company received payment in full from Lester Company. No reversing entries were prepared.

15. Repeat your answer to Question 14 assuming Melter Company did prepare reversing entries on January 1, 19X2.

16. Referring to Question 14, assume instead that Melter Company discounted the note at the bank, with recourse, on December 1, 19X1, 30 days after it had received it. The bank's discount rate was 12%. On January 30, 19X2, Melter Company received word that Lester Company had dishonored payment of the note. Melter company paid the amount due, plus a $25 protest fee to the bank. In general journal form, record the following transactions:

   a. the discounting of the note at the bank

   b. payment to the bank upon the default of Lester Company

Check Yourself

1. d **(Characteristics of short-term liquid assets)**

2. a **(Short-term marketable securities)**
   (*Note:* the correct answer was b prior to issuance of the new FASB.)

3.

		DR	CR
a.	Short Term Investments	146,000	
	Cash		146,000
b.	Short-Term Investments	125,000	
	Cash		125,000
c.	Short-Term Investments	320,000	
	Cash		320,000
d.	Cash	150,000	
	Short-Term Investments		146,000
	Interest Income		4,000
e.	Short-Term Investments	66,000	
	Cash		66,000
f.	Cash	1,700*	
	Dividend Income		1,700
g.	Cash	84,000	
	Short-Term Investments		75,000
	Gain on Sale of Short-Term Investments		9,000
h	Cash	296,000	
	Loss on Sale of Short-Term Investments	24,000	
	Short-Term Investments		320,000

*[(5,000 × $0,10) + (8,000 × $0.15) = $500 + $1,200 = $1,700]
(Short-term marketable securities— journal entries)

4. c **(Accounts receivable)**

5.

	DR	CR
a. Uncollectible Accounts Expense	146,000	
Allowance for Uncollectible Accounts		146,000

b.

Allowance for Uncollectible Accounts

	6,800	Beginning	
Write-offs 6,500	7,500	Adjustment(a)	
	7,800	Adjusted Balance	

Uncollectible Accounts Expense

Adjustment(a) 7,500	
7,500	

(Accounts receivable — journal entries and calculation of uncollectible accounts expense using the percentage of sales method)

6. a.

Age of Account	Year-end Balance of Accounts Receivable	Percentage Uncollectible	Amount Required in Allowance Account
1–30 days	$22,000	1	$220
31–60 days	38,000	2	760
61–90 days	18,000	10	1,800
over 90 days	12,000	40	4,800
	$90,000		$7,580

b. $7,580 **(Accounts receivable — preparing an aging schedule and estimating the allowance for uncollectible accounts)**

7.

		DR	CR
a.	Uncollectible Accounts Expense	7,280	
	Allowance for Uncollectible Accounts		7,280

b.

Allowance for Uncollectible Accounts					Uncollectible Accounts Expense	
		6,800	Beginning			
Write-offs	6,500	7,280	Adjustment(a)		7,280	
		7,580			7,280	

(Accounts receivable — journal entry and calculation for uncollectible accounts expense using the aging method given a debit balance in the account allowance for uncollectible accounts)

8.

		DR	CR
a.	Uncollectible Accounts Expense	7,980	
	Allowance for Uncollectible Accounts		7,980

b.

Allowance for Uncollectible Accounts					Uncollectible Accounts Expense	
		6,100	Beginning Balance			
Write-offs	6,500	7,980	Adjustment(a)	Adjustment(a)	7,980	
		7,580				

(Accounts receivable — journal entry and calculation of uncollectible accounts expense using the aging method given a debit balance in the account allowance for uncollectible accounts)

9.

	DR	CR
Allowance for Uncollectible Accounts	6,500	
Accounts Receivable		6,500

(Journal entry to write off a customer's account receivable deemed uncollectible)

10.

	DR	CR
Accounts Receivable	1,500	
Allowance for Uncollectible Accounts		1,500
Cash	1,500	
Accounts Receivable		1,500

(Journal entries to show recovery of customer account receivable previously written off)

11. b. March: 31 days – 1 day =   30 days remaining in March

April: 30 days

May   30th day

                        90 days total

(Notes receivable—short-term)

12. a. Maturity value: $9,000 + ($9,000 × .08 × 90/360) = $9,180

Bank's discount: $9,180 × .12 × 60/360 = $183.60

Cash proceeds: $9,180 – $183.60 = $8996.40

Interest expense: $8,996.40 – $9,000 = $[3.60]

(Notes receivable—short-term)

13.

		DR	CR
a.	Accounts Receivable	9,200	
	Sales		9,200
b.	Cash	4,200	
	Note Receivable	5,000	
	Accounts Receivable		9,200
c.	Cash	5,075	
	Note Receivable		5,000
	Interest Income		75

(Short-term notes receivable — journal entries)

14.

		DR	CR
a.	Note Receivable	8,000	
	Sales		8,000
b.	(Accrued) Interest Receivable	120*	
	Interest Income		120
	Interest Income	120	
	Income Summary		120

*[$8,000 × 9% or 60/360 = $120, because 60 days have elapsed since November 1.]

c.	Cash	8,180*	
	(Accrued) Interest Receivable		120
	Interest Income		60**
	Note Receivable		8,000

*[$8,000 + ($8,000 × 9% or 90/360) = $8,182]

**[$8,000 × 9% or 30/360 = $60, because 60 days have elapsed since December 31. *Hint*: review accrual-type adjusting entries.]

(Short-term notes receivable—journal entries)

15.

		DR	CR
a.	Note Receivable	8,000	
	Sales		8,000
b.	(Accrued) Interest Receivable	120	
	Interest Income		120
	Interest Income	120	
	Income Summary		120
Jan. 1	Interest Income	120	
	(Accrued) Interest Receivable		120
c.	Cash	8,180	
	Interest Income		180
	Note Receivable		8,000

(Short-term notes receivable — journal entries)

16.

		DR	CR
a.	Cash	8,016.40	
	Notes Receivable		8,000.00
	Interest Income		16.40

Maturity Value: $8,000 + ($8,000 \times .09 \times 90/360) = \$8,180$
Bank's Discount $8,180 \times .12 \times 60/360 = \$163.60$
Cash Proceeds: $8,180 - \$163.60 = \$8,016.40$
Interest Income: $8,016.40 - \$8,000 = \$16.40$

		DR	CR
b.	Accounts Receivable	8,205.00	
	Cash		8,205.00

(Short-term notes receivable—journal entries)

Grade Yourself

Circle the numbers of the questions you missed, then fill in the total incorrect for each topic. If you answered more than three questions incorrectly, you need to focus on that topic. (If a topic has less than three questions and you had at least one wrong, we suggest you study that topic also. Read your textbook, a review book, or ask your teacher for help.)

Subject: Short-Term Liquid Assets

Topic	Question Numbers	Number Incorrect
Characteristics of short-term liquid assets	1	
Short-term marketable securities	2	
Short-term marketable securities — journal entries	3	
Accounts receivable	4	
Accounts receivable — journal entries and calculation of uncollectible accounts expense using the percentage of sales method	5	
Accounts receivable — preparing an aging schedule and estimating the allowance for uncollectible accounts	6	
Accounts receivable — journal entry and calculation for uncollectible accounts expense using the aging method given a debit balance in the account allowance for uncollectible accounts	7	
Accounts receivable — preparing an aging schedule and estimating the allowance for uncollectible accounts	8	
Accounts receivable — journal entry and calculation of uncollectible accounts expense using the aging method given a debit balance in the account allowance for uncollectible accounts	9	
Journal entries to show recovery of customer account receivable previously written off	10	
Notes receivable — short term	11, 12	
Short-term notes receivable — journal entries	13, 14, 15, 16	

Inventory

8

 ## Brief Yourself

Chapter 5 provided some introductory topics relating to merchandise inventory. In this chapter we examine the accounting treatment of merchandise inventory in greater detail. We consider the effect of changing prices on *ending inventory* balances and on *cost of goods sold*. We address losses in inventory values and inventory systems. Finally, we examine methods to estimate ending inventory balances.

The inventory cost pertaining to the *units sold* is referred to as *cost of goods sold*. This amount is deducted from sales revenue on the *income statement* to determine net income.

The inventory cost attached to the *units unsold* is carried on the *balance sheet* as *assets* since it is available as a resource, or a future source of revenue to the company.

The effect of *inventory errors* can be summarized in the following four statements:

> If *ending inventory* is *overstated*, then *net income* is *overstated*.
> If *ending inventory* is *understated*, then *net income* is *understated*.
>
> If *beginning inventory* is *overstated*, then *net income* is *understated*.
> If *beginning inventory* is *understated*, then *net income* is *overstated*.

These statements refer to a two-year sequence. If no new errors are made at the end of year two, then the balance sheet accounts, inventory, and owner's capital will be correctly stated. The net income amounts reported at the end of each years, one and two, will be incorrect. However, the sum of the two years' net income will be the same as if they had been reported correctly.

Specific identification, as the name suggests, matches precisely those units sold and those units in ending inventory. Matching serial numbers is one means to accomplish this. This method is the most time-consuming of the four, and would not be recommended in settings with a high volume of low value items.

In the *(weighted) average* method, the *cost of goods available for sale* is divided by the *total units available* to determine an average unit cost.

FIFO and *LIFO* are acronyms that stand for *first in, first out* and *last in, first out*, respectively. FIFO describes a situation in which the first units acquired are the first units sold. So the last units acquired remain in ending inventory. LIFO describes a situation in which the last units acquired are the first units sold. So the first units acquired remain in ending inventory.

The following formula may be useful in solving questions about assigning cost to ending inventory and cost of goods sold:

	Beginning inventory
+	Net Purchases
=	Cost of Goods Available
−	Ending inventory
=	Cost of Goods Sold

If the problem asks you to solve for ending inventory under FIFO, then look at the last units acquired as the ending inventory. If the problem asks you to solve for Cost of Goods Sold under FIFO, solve for the ending inventory first, then deduct from cost of goods available, to arrive at the answer, cost of goods sold.

If the problem asks you to solve for ending inventory under LIFO, then look at the first units acquired as the ending inventory. If the problem asks you to solve for Cost of Goods Sold under LIFO, solve for the ending inventory first, then deduct from cost of goods available, to arrive at the answer, cost of goods sold.

In times of rising prices, LIFO yields a lower net income amount and a lower tax liability, because the cost of goods sold would be higher. LIFO better matches cost of goods sold with replacement cost. The disadvantage of LIFO is that Inventory on the Balance Sheet would be understated.

The physical flow of goods need not match the inventory valuation method. In other words, you may sell the oldest first and still use LIFO.

In the *perpetual* inventory system, the Inventory account is debited whenever an increase in inventory occurs, and is credited whenever a decrease occurs. This system results in an Inventory account balance that is always up to date.

The *periodic* inventory system bypasses the Inventory account until the end of the accounting period. In the interim, the Purchases account is used for acquisitions of new inventory. At the end of the period, the inventory is physically counted, and the account balance is updated either with adjusting or with closing entries.

The *Lower-of-Cost-or-Market* rule is an application of the *conservatism* convention. If market value is lower than cost, an adjustment for the loss in value is recorded and reported in the accounting period when the decline occurred.

Although taking a physical inventory count is the most accurate means of determining ending inventory, there are circumstances when estimating inventory may be appropriate. Companies that use the periodic inventory system must estimate ending inventory for interim financial reporting when a taking a physical count is too costly and too disruptive to business. Companies that suffer inventory losses due to natural disasters such as floods, tornadoes, etc., may need to rely on estimates of inventory to file insurance claims. A company that suspects theft of inventory may wish to take an actual physical inventory, then compare that amount to an estimate. If a significant difference occurs, its suspicions may be correct.

Two means of estimating ending inventory are the *gross profit* method and the *retail inventory* method.

Test Yourself

1. The cost of inventory is deducted from revenue on the income statement when:

   a. it is received.

   b. it is paid for.

   c. it is sold.

   d. the proceeds from sales are collected.

2. If merchandise held on consignment is erroneously included in the count of the ending inventory, what is the result?

   a. Net income is overstated.

   b. Net income is not affected this year, but it will be overstated next year.

   c. Net income is understated.

   d. Owner's equity is understated.

3. Little Company reported net income of $21,000 in 19X1 and $27,000 in 19X2. During 19X3 it discovered that the 19X1 ending inventory had been understated by $3,000. That was the only inventory error made.

   a. Calculate the corrected net income amounts for 19X1 and 19X2.

   b. What effect, if any, will there be on the 19X3 beginning general ledger balances?

4. Which inventory valuation method best matches cost of goods sold with current replacement cost?

   a. specific identification

   b. FIFO

   c. LIFO

   d. weighted average

5. Which inventory valuation method best matches ending inventory with current replacement cost?

   a. specific identification

   b. FIFO

   c. LIFO

   d. weighted average

6. During inflationary times, which inventory method yields the lowest tax liability?

   a. specific identification

   b. FIFO

   c. LIFO

   d. weighted average

7. Adamski Company had information available about its beginning inventory and subsequent purchases during the year. That information is detailed in the schedule below. Adamski Company sold 200 units during the year at a selling price of $50 each. Using the FIFO, LIFO, and weighted average methods:

   a. compute the cost allocated to ending inventory and cost of goods sold, and;

   b. compute the amount of the gross margin.

	units	cost
Beginning inventory	20	$20
Purchase February	22	$21
Purchase March	24	$23
Purchase April	21	$22
Purchase May	23	$24
Purchase June	25	$26
Purchase July	20	$25
Purchase August	22	$24
Purchase September	21	$27
Purchase October	23	$28
Purchase November	24	$29
Purchase December	25	$30

8. The following data pertain to the inventory of King Company.

Item	Quantity in Units	Unit Cost	Unit Market
Category I			
M	100	$5.00	$4.80
N	150	4.50	4.60
O	125	4.00	3.90
Category II			
P	75	$8.00	$7.75
Q	50	6.00	6.50

Compute the inventory valuation applying the lower-of-cost-or-market rule under each of the following methods:

a. item by item

b. major category

c. total inventory

9. Referring to Question 8, choose the method that requires the largest lower-of-cost-or-market inventory adjustment and prepare the balance sheet presentation that would result.

10. Flooding and high winds during a 19X5 hurricane destroyed all the inventory in the warehouse of Peachdelight Clothing Distributors. The contents of the inventory in the showroom remained undamaged, due primarily to its location on higher ground. A physical inventory taken the day after the hurricane subsided revealed undamaged inventory costing $1500.00. Peachdelight Clothing maintains a periodic inventory system, so it does not have a detailed record of its current-year cost of sales. However, it consistently maintains a 40% gross profit ratio to sales; sales for the current year were $80,000. Other records retrieved from a safe location revealed the following data:

Ending inventory December 31, 19X4	$1,000.00
Purchases of merchandise during 19X5	65,000.00
Purchase returns	6,000.00
Freight-in	1,000.00

Calculate the estimated inventory loss from the hurricane so that Peachdelight can file an insurance claim.

11. Reardon's Furniture Store uses the retail inventory method to estimate its interim inventory balance. It has the following data available:

Beginning inventory (at cost)	$40,000
Beginning inventory (at retail)	75,000
Freight-in	5,000
Net purchases (at cost)	87,000
Net purchases (at retail)	145,000
Sales	175,000

Calculate the estimated ending inventory at cost of Reardon's Furniture Store using the retail inventory method.

Check Yourself

1. c: the matching rule (**The effect of inventory cost in determining net income**)

2. a: Overstated ending inventory results in overstated net income. (**The effect of inventory cost in determining net income**)

3. a. Understated ending inventory results in understated net income.
    Understated beginning inventory results in overstated net income.

	Reported			Corrected
19X1	$21,000	+ 3,000	=	$24,000
19X2	27,000	− 3,000	=	$24,000
	$48,000		=	$48,000

    b. If no new error is made at the end of 19X5, then inventory and owner's capital general ledger balances will be correct. (**The effect of inventory cost in determining net income**)

4. c (**Assigning cost to ending inventory and cost of goods sold**)

5. b (**Assigning cost to ending inventory and cost of goods sold**)

6. c (**Assigning cost to ending inventory and cost of goods sold**)

7. a. Schedule of Cost of Goods Available for Sale

Beginning	20 @	$20	= $400
February	22 @	$21	= $462
March	24 @	$23	= $552
April	21 @	$22	= $462
May	23 @	$24	= $552
June	25 @	$26	= $650
July	20 @	$25	= $500
August	22 @	$24	= $528
September	21 @	$27	= $567
October	23 @	$28	= $644
November	24 @	$29	= $696
December	25 @	$30	= $750
Cost of Goods Available for Sale	270		$6,763

    If 270 units were available and 200 units were sold, then 70 units were available in ending inventory.

7. (*continued*)

    Ending Inventory and Cost of Goods Sold under FIFO, LIFO, and Weighted Average Methods

<u>FIFO</u>

Cost of Goods Available			$6,763
Ending Inventory	December	25 @ $30 = $750	
	November	24 @ $29 = $696	
	October	21 @ $28 = $<u>588</u>	$<u>2,034</u>
Cost of Goods Sold			$<u>4,729</u>

<u>LIFO</u>

Cost of Goods Available			$6,763
Ending Inventory	Beginning	20 @ $20 = $400	
	February	22 @ $21 = $462	
	March	24 @ $23 = $552	
	April	4 @ $22 = $<u>88</u>	<u>1,502</u>
Cost of Goods Sold			$<u>5,261</u>

<u>Weighted Average</u>

Cost of Goods Available		$6,763
Ending Inventory	70 @ $25.05* = $1,753.50	$<u>1,754</u> (rounded)
Cost of Goods Sold		$<u>5,009</u>

$*(\dfrac{Cost\ of\ Goods\ Available}{Units\ Available} = Weighted\ Average\ Cost\ per\ Unit)$

$[\dfrac{\$6,763}{270} = \$25.05(rounded)]$

b. Gross Margin under FIFO, LIFO, and Weighted Average Methods

	FIFO	LIFO	Weighted Average
Sales (200 @ $50)	$10,000	$10,000	$10,000
Cost of Goods Sold	<u>4,729</u>	<u>5,261</u>	<u>5,009</u>
Gross Margins	$5,271	$4,739	$4,991

(Assigning cost to ending inventory and cost of goods sold)

8. a. item by item

Item	Quantity in Units	Unit Cost	Unit Market	Total Cost	Total Market	Lower of Cost or Market
Category I						
M	100	$5.00	$4.80	$500.00	$480.00	$480.00
N	150	4.50	4.60	675.00	690.00	675.00
O	125	4.00	3.90	500.00	487.50	487.50
Category II						
P	75	$8.00	$7.75	600.00	$581.25	581.25
Q	50	6.00	6.50	300.00	325.00	<u>300.00</u>
						<u>$2,523.75</u>

b. major category

Item	Quantity in Units	Unit Cost	Unit Market	Total Cost	Total Market	Lower of Cost or Market
Category I						
M	100	$5.00	$4.80	$500.00	$480.00	
N	150	4.50	4.60	675.00	690.00	
O	125	4.00	3.90	<u>500.00</u>	<u>487.50</u>	
				<u>$1,675.00</u>	<u>$1,657.50</u>	$1,657.50
Category II						
P	75	$8.00	$7.75	600.00	$581.25	
Q	50	6.00	6.50	<u>300.00</u>	<u>325.00</u>	
				<u>$900.00</u>	$906.25	<u>900.00</u>
						<u>$2,557.50</u>

8. (*continued*) c. total inventory

Item	Quantity in Units	Unit Cost	Unit Market	Total Cost	Total Market	Lower of Cost or Market
Category I						
M	100	$5.00	$4.80	$500.00	$480.00	
N	150	4.50	4.60	675.00	690.00	
O	125	4.00	3.90	500.00	487.50	
Category II						
P	75	$8.00	$7.50	600.00	$581.25	
Q	50	6.00	6.50	300.00	325.00	
				$2,575.00	$2,563.75	2,563.75

(Applying the lower-of-cost-or-market rule to inventory)

9. The largest lower-of-cost-or-market inventory adjustment would occur with the item-by-item method (a), since the increased value of some items cannot offset the lower value of other items.

Assets	
Cash	$XXXX
Accounts Receivable	XXXX
Inventory (at lower-of-cost-or-market; cost is $2,575)	2,523.75

(Applying the lower-of-cost-or-market rule to inventory)

10.

Sales	$80,000.00	100.0%
Cost of Goods Sold (estimated)	<u>48,000.00</u>	<u>60.0%</u>
Gross Profit	<u>$32,000.00</u>	40.0%
Beginning inventory 19X5	$1,000.00	
Purchases	65,000.00	
less: Purchase returns	(6,000.00)	
add: Freight-in	<u>1,000.00</u>	
Cost of Goods Available for Sale	$61,000.00	
less: Cost of Goods Sold (estimated)	<u>48,000.00</u>	
Inventory on hand at the time of the hurricane	$13,000.00	
less: Inventory undamaged	<u>1,500.00</u>	
Inventory loss	<u>$11,500.00</u>	

(Estimating inventory — gross profit method)

11.

	Cost	Retail
Beginning inventory	$40,000	$75,000
Net Purchases (at cost)	87,000	
Freight-in	5,000	
Net Purchases (at retail)	_____	<u>145,000</u>
Goods available	$132,000	$220,000

Ratio of cost to retail price: $132,000/$220,000 = 60.0%		
Net Sales during the Period		<u>175,000</u>
Estimated Ending Inventory (at retail)		<u>$45,000</u>
Estimated Ending Inventory (at cost: $45,000 x 60.0%)		<u>$27,000</u>

(Estimating inventory — retail inventory method)

Grade Yourself

Circle the numbers of the questions you missed, then fill in the total incorrect for each topic. If you answered more than three questions incorrectly, you need to focus on that topic. (If a topic has less than three questions and you had at least one wrong, we suggest you study that topic also. Read your textbook, a review book, or ask your teacher for help.)

Subject: Inventory

Topic	Question Numbers	Number Incorrect
The effect of inventory cost in determining net income	1, 2, 3	
Assigning cost to ending inventory and cost of goods sold	4, 5, 6, 7	
Applying the lower-of-cost-or-market rule to inventory	8, 9	
Estimating inventory—gross profit method	10	
Estimating inventory—retail inventory method	11	

Current Liabilities

9

Brief Yourself

In this chapter our attention turns to the subject of current liabilities. We address classification issues relating to current liabilities and examine journal entries pertaining to current liabilities.

A liability is classified as current if it is to be satisfied within one year or an operating cycle, whichever is the longer of the two.

Current liabilities may be classified in one of three categories:

   1) definitely determinable

   2) estimated

   3) contingent

Definitely determinable liabilities are those that are certain and for which the precise amount can be calculated. Examples include notes payable (short term), interest payable, and sales taxes payable.

Estimated liabilities are those that are certain, but for which the amount cannot be precisely calculated. To honor the *matching principle*, the liability is recorded as an estimated amount. Examples include:

   1) product warranty liabilities

   2) vacation pay liabilities

Contingent liabilities are *potential* liabilities that arose from an event that has already occurred, but has not been resolved. Some contingent liabilities are recorded; others are merely mentioned in the notes to the financial statements. The selection of an appropriate accounting treatment is determined by factors such as probability of outcome and the ability to estimate the liability. Very often legal counsel is consulted before an accounting treatment is selected.

Payroll accounting involves establishing current liabilities. Federal, state, and local taxes withheld from employees' gross earnings, and payroll taxes that are the responsibility of the employer must be recorded in separate current liability accounts.

 # Test Yourself

1. The best definition for a current liability is:

   a. an obligation that must be satisfied during the upcoming year or operating cycle, whichever is the longer period of time.

   b. an obligation incurred within the past year.

   c. an obligation currently on the books.

   d. Both (b) and (c) are correct.

2. Of the following liabilities, which would most likely be classified as current?

   a. mortgage payable

   b. bonds payable

   c. note payable (due in five years)

   d. property taxes payable

3. If current liabilities are understated on the balance sheet, what other category on the financial statements is probably misstated?

   a. current assets

   b. revenues

   c. expenses

   d. Nothing else is necessarily misstated.

4. Which of the following liabilities is an example of one that is most probably estimated?

   a. interest payable

   b. FICA taxes payable

   c. accounts payable

   d. vacation wages payable

5. Which of the following situations is an example of a contingent liability?

   a. A bank loan officer is expected to respond within the next 48 hours regarding a loan application.

   b. A customer has filed a lawsuit regarding an alleged product-related injury; the scheduled court date is four months from now.

   c. An examination of the past five years of product warranty claims reveals an average replacement rate of 1%.

   d. The city council is meeting next week; on its calendar is a vote on whether to raise the property tax rate for next year.

6. Michelle Martin has purchased new testing equipment costing $12,000 for Environmental Testing Services. She has financed 100% of the purchase by issuing a 90-day, 9% interest-bearing note to her neighborhood credit union on March 1. Environmental Testing Services prepares quarterly financial statements. The end of the first quarter is March 31.

   a. Prepare the following transactions for Environmental Testing Services in general journal form, without reversing entries:

   March 1   The issuance of the note to the neighborhood credit union.

   March 31   The accrual for the quarter-end interest on the note.

   March 31   The closing entry for the quarter-end interest.

   May 30   The repayment of the note to the credit union.

b. Prepare the transactions in Question 6a above in general journal form; however, include the reversing entry option on April 1.

7. Referring to Question 6a, prepare the current liabilities section of the balance sheet for Environmental Testing Services for March 31.

8. On August 31, 19X5, Lucács Company discounted a 90-day, $12,000 note at the bank at 9%. Lucács Company prepares quarterly financial statements. The end of its third quarter is September 30. Record the following in general journal form:

August 31	The note was discounted at the bank.
September 30	The third-quarter adjusting and closing entries are prepared.
November 29	The note is repaid to the bank.

9. Referring to Question 8, show the current liability section of the balance sheet of Lucács Company on September 30, 1995.

10. Lanier Pharmacy is located in Fulton County where a 6% sales tax is levied on all sales transactions. The sales tax return must be filed by the 20th day of the following month, along with the release of the funds to the state. The gross receipts, which include the sales tax, were $90,100 for the month of December. In general journal form, record:

a. in summary, the sales and sales tax for the month;

b. the payment of the sales tax to the state the following month.

11. The Newcom Company guarantees its products by offering to replace defective units within one year of purchase. In the past, on average, 1% of units sold have been replaced. The inventory cost of each unit is $42, and the selling price of each unit is $70. In September, Newcom Company sold 10,000 units and replaced 105 units under warranty. In general journal form, record the September transactions pertaining to the product warranties.

12. Rose Garcia is paid at a regular rate of $15 per hour for work up to forty hours per week, and 150% of the regular rate for work over forty hours during a week. During the week of August 1, 19X5, Rose worked forty-eight hours. The combined rate for withholding of Social Security and Medicare taxes is 7.65%. Other withholdings are $55 for federal income taxes, $12 for state income taxes, and $28 for health insurance.

Rose's employer, Hope Industries, must pay its share of the Social Security and Medicare taxes at a total rate of 7.65%, as well as state unemployment taxes of 5.4% and federal unemployment taxes of 0.8%. Calculate each of the following amounts:

a. Rose's gross wages for the week of August 1, 1995

b. Rose's net take-home pay for the week of August 1, 1995

c. Hope Industries' payroll tax expense for Rose for the week of August 1, 19X5

d. The credits to the various payroll taxes payable accounts

Check Yourself

1. a **(Characteristics of current liabilities)**

2. d **(Characteristics of current liabilities)**

3. c **(Characteristics of current liabilities)**

4. d **(Characteristics of current liabilities)**

5. b **(Characteristics of current liabilities)**

6 a.

		DR	CR
March 1	Testing Equipment	12,000	
	Note Payable		12,000
March 31	Interest Expense	90	
	Accrued Interest Payable ($12,000 \times 0.09 \times 30/360$)		90
March 31	Income Summary	90	
	Interest Expense		90
May 30	Note Payable	12,000	
	Interest Expense ($12,000 \times 0.09 \times 60/360$)	180	
	Accrued Interest Payable	90	

6. b.

			DR	CR
March 1	Testing Equipment		12,000	
	Note Payable			12,000
March 31	Interest Expense		90	
	Accrued Interest Payable			90
	($12,000 × 0.09 × 30/360)			
March 31	Income Summary		90	
	Interest Expense			90
April 1	Accrued Interest Payable		90	
	Interest Expense			90
May 30	Note Payable		12,000	
	Interest Expense		270	
	Cash			12,270

(Notes payable — short-term)

7.

Environmental Testing Services
Balance Sheet
March 31, 19X5

Current Liabilities	
Accrued Interest Payable	$90
Note Payable (due May 30, 19X5)	12,000
Total Current Liabilities	$12,090

(Notes payable — short-term)

8.

				DR	CR
August	31	Cash		11,730	
		Discount on Note Payable		270	
		Note Payable			12,000
September	30	Interest Expense		90	
		Discount on Note Payable			90
	30	Income Summary		90	
		Interest Expense			90
November	29	Note Payable		12,000	
		Interest Expense		180	
		Cash			12,000
		Discount on Note Payable			180

(Notes payable — short-term)

9.

Lukács Company
Balance Sheet
September 30, 19X5

Current Liabilities

Note Payable (due November 29, 19X5)	$12,000	
less: Discount on Note Payable	180	
Note Payable, net	$11,820	

(Notes payable — short-term)

10.

		DR	CR
a.	Cash	90,100	
	Sales		85,000
	Sales Taxes Payable		51,000
b.	Sales Taxes Payable	5,100	
	Cash		51,00

(Current liabilities — definitely determinable)

11.

	DR	CR
Product Warranty Expense (10,000 × 0.01 × $42)	4,200	
Estimated Product Warranty Liability		4,200
Estimated Product Warranty Liability (105 x $42)	4,410	
Inventory		4,410

(Estimated liabilities)

12. a.   (40 × $15) + (8 × $15 × 150%) = $780

    b. $780 − [(7.65% × $780) + $55 + $12 + $28] = $780 − $154.67 = $625.33

    c.   (7.65% + 5.4% + 0.8%)$780 = 13.85% × $780 = $108.03

    d.   Social Security and Medicare taxes payable

Employer's share	$59.67	
Employee's share	59.67	$119.34
Federal income tax withholdings payable		55.00
State income tax withholdings payable		12.00
State unemployment taxes payable ($780 × 5.4%)		42.12
Federal unemployment taxes payable ($700 × 0.8%)		6.24

(Payroll accounting)

Grade Yourself

Circle the numbers of the questions you missed, then fill in the total incorrect for each topic. If you answered more than three questions incorrectly, you need to focus on that topic. (If a topic has less than three questions and you had at least one wrong, we suggest you study that topic also. Read your textbook, a review book, or ask your teacher for help.)

Subject: Current Liabilities

Topic	Question Numbers	Number Incorrect
Characteristics of current liabilities	1, 2, 3, 4, 5	
Notes payable — short-term	6, 7, 8, 9, 10	
Estimated liabilities	11	
Payroll accounting	12	

Property, Plant, and Equipment: Acquisition and Depreciation

 Brief Yourself

This chapter is the first of three chapters that shift our attention to long-term assets. Long-term assets first may be divided into two groups, *tangible* and *intangible*. Tangible refers to those assets that have physical properties. This category generally is subdivided into specific groups such as *property, plant, and equipment* and *natural resources*. Examples of each group follow:

Tangible		Intangible
property, plant, and equipment	**natural resources**	
land	timberlands	patents
buildings	oil and gas fields	franchises
vehicles	gravel pits	trademarks
machinery	iron ore mines	copyrights
furniture		goodwill

In this chapter we will focus on property, plant, and equipment. In a subsequent chapter we will focus on natural resources and intangible assets.

The *cost* of property, plant, and equipment very often includes more elements than the purchase price. The following items are a sampling of factors to consider when determining the accounting cost:

Land	Land Improvements	Buildings	Machinery
purchase price	fences	purchase price	purchase price
back taxes owed by	outdoor lighting	renovation	freight-in
seller	signage	architect's fee	installation
grading	outdoor sprinklers		special base
landscaping	paving of parking lot		testing
clearing sewer lines			
attorney fees			
real estate fee			

Property, plant, and equipment, *except land*, are depreciated. The accounting definition of *depreciation* includes the concept of the allocation of the cost of an asset to the accounting periods which are served by the use of an asset. To define depreciation merely as a decline in the value of an asset falls short of the accounting definition.

The factors that affect the depreciation computation are: 1) cost; 2) residual value; 3) depreciable cost; and 4) estimated useful life. Residual value, also referred to as salvage or scrap value, is an estimated amount; the depreciable cost is simply the cost less the residual value—in other words, the total amount to be depreciated; the estimated useful life is measured in years or in activity units, such as total miles driven or total productive hours.

To record depreciation, use the journal entry illustrated in Chapter 3:

> Depreciation Expense   xx
>   Accumulated Depreciation   xx

The balance in the depreciation expense account shows only the current period depreciation. It is reported on the income statement, and its balance is closed to income summary each year. The accumulated depreciation account is a contra asset account to the specific asset. Its balance contains the total depreciation taken on an asset from the very beginning. It is reported on the balance sheet in the asset section as a subtraction from the specific asset to which it pertains. The cost of an asset less any balance in the accumulated depreciation account is referred to as the *carrying value*.

To compute depreciation under the *straight-line method*, use the following formula:

$$\frac{Cost - Residual\,Value}{Estimated\,Useful\,Life}$$

The base (denominator) for the straight-line method is expressed in years or in months.

If the depreciable item is purchased after the beginning of a year, a *partial year's* depreciation must be calculated for the first year. For the straight-line method, begin with the preceding formula and insert a fraction of the year as a multiplier. For instance, if an item is placed into use on March 2, calculate the straight-line depreciation as before, then multiply times 10/12, because the item will be used 10 months out of 12 in the first year. Subsequent years' depreciation are calculated as full years, with the final year resulting in another partial year calculation, because it extends over into an additional calendar year. The depreciation amount extending into the final calendar year would be calculated using a 2/12 multiplier.

The *sum-of-the-year's-digits* method of depreciation is one type of accelerated depreciation. In other words, the most depreciation is applied to the first year, with less applied to each subsequent year. A fraction must be calculated based on a formula, then applied as a multiplier to the depreciable amount. The denominator of the fraction is calculated by creating a sum of the digits of the number of years of useful life. For example, if an item is estimated to have a four-year useful life, the accountant would calculate the denominator as 10 from the sum of $1 + 2 + 3 + 4$. An alternative calculation may be used for the denominator. That is $n(n+1)/2$, where n is set equal to the number of years of useful life; in this example $n = 4$. So, $4(4+1)/2 = 10$.

The numerator of the fraction is the number of years of remaining useful life at the beginning of the year. Accordingly, in year one, the fraction would be 4/10; in year two, it would be 3/10; in year three, it would be 2/10; in year four, it would be 1/10.

To compute depreciation using the *production method*, use the following formula:

$$\frac{(Current\ year\ actual\ activity)}{(Total\ estimated\ activity)} \times (Cost - Residual\ Value)$$

(Current year actual activity)

(Total estimated activity) × (Cost – Residual Value)

To compute depreciation using the *double-declining balance method*, use the following formula:

Carrying value at the beginning of the year × straight-line rate × 2

The *straight-line rate* formula is 1/Estimated Useful Life. The carrying value in year one is the *full cost*, NOT the cost less the residual value. Repeat the equation each year. Only the carrying value will decrease (see definition above). For the final year of depreciation, throw away the formula and calculate the depreciation as *the carrying value less the residual value*.

Revised depreciation may be required if, based on new information, the useful life of the item is shorter. The key to revise depreciation is to calculate the remaining depreciable amount over the remaining number of years of useful life.

Test Yourself

1. Expenditures for property, plant, and equipment are charged to long-term asset accounts because of which underlying principle?

   a. the matching rule

   b. the cost-benefit rule

   c. the conservatism rule

   d. all of the above

2. Which of the following costs would not be charged to the Land account?

   a. tearing down an old building

   b. the attorney's fee at closing

   c. paying the outstanding property taxes left unpaid by the seller

   d. paving the parking lot

3. Vivian Soules, M.D. purchases land and a building to establish a new inner-city medical clinic. The total cost is $100,000. The land has a fair market value of $50,000, and the building has a fair market value of $75,000. The land and building should be recorded at:

   a. $62,500 each.

   b. $50,000 and $75,000, respectively.

   c. $40,000 and $60,000, respectively.

   d. $50,000 each.

4. The best accounting definition for depreciation of an asset emphasizes:

   a. the physical deterioration of the asset.

   b. the allocation of the cost of the asset.

   c. the loss in market value of the asset.

   d. the gradual obsolescence of the asset.

5. A graph depicting accelerated depreciation would contain a line:

   a. extending straight horizontally from left to right.

   b. slanting upward extending from left to right

   c. slanting downward extending from left to right

   d. extending vertically

6. Michelle Martin purchased a new truck for Environmental Testing Services on January 2. The truck cost $19,000. She estimates that it has a useful life of five years and that its residual value at the end of that time will be $1,000. She further estimates that the truck will be driven a total of 200,000 miles. The actual miles the truck was driven during years one through three are 40,000, 45,000, and 42,000, respectively. Calculate the depreciation for the first three years using each of the depreciation methods:

   a. straight-line

   b. double-declining balance

   c. sum-of-the-years-digits

   d. units of production

7. Referring to Question 6, calculate the accumulated depreciation balance and the carrying value for the first three years using each of the depreciation methods:

   a. straight-line

   b. double-declining balance

   c. sum-of-the-years-digits

   d. units of production

8. Referring to Question 6a, assume instead that the truck was purchased on March 2. Calculate the depreciation for the first year using the straight-line method.

9. When Judy Grant, M.D., established her medical practice, she purchased an X-ray machine for $355,000. Originally, the machine was estimated to have a useful life of ten years with a residual value of $5,000. The machine was depreciated for five years using the straight-line method. At the beginning of the seventh year, it became apparent that, due to new technology, the machine would be useful only for another two years. The residual value remained unchanged. Calculate the depreciation for the seventh and eighth years.

Check Yourself

1. a. The expense is matched to the period in which the asset helps generate revenue. (**Classification of property, plant, and equipment**)

2. d. The parking lot deteriorates with time and usage; thus, the cost should be charged to the Land Improvements account so that it can be depreciated. (**Classification of property, plant, and equipment**)

3. c. $50,000 + $75,000 = $125,000; $50,000/$125,000 = 40% percentage of total fair market value pertaining to land;
$75,000/$125,000 = 60% percentage of total fair market value pertaining to building;
$100,000 × 40% = $40,000 land percentage applied to cost;
$100,000 × 60% = $60,000 building percentage applied to cost.
(**Acquisition of property, plant, and equipment**)

4. b. (**Depreciation — characteristics**)

5. c. (**Depreciation — characteristics**)

6. a. $\dfrac{\$19,000 - \$1,000}{5 \text{ years}} = \$3,600 \text{ each year}$

   b. year 1: $19,000 × 1/5 x 2 = $7,600

   year 2:   ($19,000 – $7,600) × 1/5 x 2 = $4,560

   year 3:   ($19,000 – $7,600 – $4,560) × 1/5 × 2 = $2,736

   c. Denominator: 1 + 2 + 3 + 4 + 5 = 15, or

   using n(n+1)/2 when n = 5:5(5+1)/2 = 15

   year 1:   5/15 × ($19,000 – $1,000) = $6,000

   year 2:   4/15 × ($19,000 – $1,000) = $4,800

   year 3:   3/15 × ($19,000 – $1,000) = $3,600

   d. rate per mile $= \dfrac{(\$19,000 - \$1,000)}{200,000 \text{ miles}} = \$0.09$

   year 1: 40,000 miles × $0.09 = $3,600

   year 2: 45,000 miles × $0.09 = $4,050

   year 3: 42,000 miles × $0.09 = $3,780

   OR

   year 1: 40,000 miles/200,000 miles × ($19,000 – $1,000) = $3,600

   year 2: 45,000 miles/200,000 miles × ($19,000 – $1,000) = $4,050

   year 3: 42.000 miles/200,000 miles × ($19,000 – $1,000) = $3,780

   (**Depreciation — calculation**)

7.

			Accumulated Depreciation	Carrying Value
				costs – accumulated depreciation = carrying value
a.	year 1:		$3,600	$19,000 – 3,600 = 15,400
	year 2:	$3,600 + 3,600	$7,200	$19,000 – 7,200 = $11,800
	year 3:	$3,600 3,600 + 3,600	$10,800	$19,000 – 10,800 = $8,200
b.	year 1:		$7,600	$19,000 – $7,600 = $11,400
	year 2:	$7,600 + 4,560	$12,160	$19,000 – 12,160 = $6,840
	year 3:	$7,600 4,560 + 2,736	$14,896	$19,000 – 14,896 = $4,104
c.	year 1:		$6,000	$19,000 – 6,000 = $13,000
	year 2:	$6,000 + 4,800	$10,800	$19,000 – 14,400 = 8,200
	year 3:	$6,000 4,800 + 3,600	$14,400	$19,000 – 10,800 = $4,600
d.	year 1:		$3,600	$19,000 – 3,600 =$15,400
	year 2:	$3,600 + 4,050	$7,650	$19,000 – 7,650 = 11,350
	year 3:	$3,600 4,050 + 3,780	$11,430	$19,000 – 11,430 = $7,570

(Accumulated depreciation and carrying value of asset)

8. $\dfrac{(\$19{,}000 - \$1{,}000)}{5 \text{ years}} \times \dfrac{10}{12} = \$3{,}000$ **(Depreciation)**

9. years 1 through 5: $\dfrac{(\$355{,}000 - \$5{,}000)}{10 \text{ years}} = \$35{,}000$ per year for 6 years

    6 years x $35,000 = $210,000

    $\dfrac{(\$355{,}000 - \$5{,}000 - \$210{,}000)}{2 \text{ years}} = \$70{,}000$ per year for two years

    (Revised depreciation)

Grade Yourself

Circle the numbers of the questions you missed, then fill in the total incorrect for each topic. If you answered more than three questions incorrectly, you need to focus on that topic. (If a topic has less than three questions and you had at least one wrong, we suggest you study that topic also. Read your textbook, a review book, or ask your teacher for help.)

Subject: Property, Plant, and Equipment: Acquisition and Depreciation

Topic	Question Numbers	Number Incorrect
Classification of property, plant, and equipment	1, 2	
Acquisition of property, plant, and equipment	3	
Depreciation — characteristics	4, 5	
Depreciation — calculation	6, 8	
Accumulated depreciation and carrying value of asset	7	
Revised depreciation	9	

Property, Plant, and Equipment: Additional Expenditures, Disposals, and Exchanges

Brief Yourself

In this chapter we continue our focus on property, plant, and equipment. We examine the accounting treatment of additional expenditures for property, plant, and equipment, such as for routine repairs, extraordinary repairs, additions, and betterments; we consider the matching rule when choosing the appropriate accounting treatment. We also examine disposals and exchanges of property, plant, and equipment.

If the benefit of an additional expenditure extends beyond the current accounting period, then that cost should be charged to an asset account. We refer to this as a *capital expenditure*. The additional cost will result in either larger amounts of depreciation or in extended years of depreciation. If the benefit of the additional expenditure expires within the current accounting period, then the amount of the expenditure should be charged to an expense account. We refer to this as a *revenue expenditure*, because the expense is deducted from the current period's revenues.

A key factor to emphasize for journal entries to record the disposal of property, plant, and equipment is that the asset account and the related account accumulated depreciation each contain an amount pertaining to the item being disposed. Accordingly, the journal entry must include a debit to the accumulated depreciation account and a credit to the asset account. This combination will be the core of the journal entry, no matter whether the item is sold for cash at a loss, or whether the item is discarded. Be familiar with the following journal entry models:

	DR	CR
Accumulated Depreciation — Equipment	xx	
Loss on Disposal of Equipment	xx	
Equipment (to record discarding of equipment)		xx
Accumulated Depreciation — Equipment	xx	
Cash	xx	
Equipment (to record sale of equipment for a cash amount equal to the carrying value—that is, no gain or loss)		xx
Accumulated Depreciation — Equipment	xx	
Cash	xx	
Loss on sale of Equipment	xx	
Equipment (to record sale of equipment for a cash amount less than the carrying value—that is, a loss)		xx
Accumulated Depreciation - Equipment	xx	
Cash	xx	
Gain on Sale of Equipment		xx
Equipment (to record sale of equipment for a cash amount greater than the carrying value—that is, a gain)		xx

To record journal entries for exchanges of property, two additional factors must be considered before completion. One is the amount of the trade-in allowance granted by the merchant. The other is whether the exchange of the old asset is for a dissimilar (unlike) asset, or for a similar (like) asset.

If the trade-in allowance is greater than the carrying value of the old asset, a gain is realized. If the trade-in allowance is less than the carrying value of the old asset, a loss is realized. If the assets being exchanged are *dissimilar*, then realized gains and losses are recorded. According to income tax rules, if the assets being exchanged are *similar*, gains and losses are not recognized. Instead, the cost basis of the new asset is adjusted.

Test Yourself

1. Match each term with its corresponding definition below. Use each term only once.

   a. Revenue expenditure

   b. Capital expenditure

   c. Addition

   d. Betterment

   e. Extraordinary repair

   f. Ordinary repair

   i. The routine cost to maintain or make a minor repair on a piece of equipment, such as a regular tune-up. _____

   ii. The cost of enlarging a facility, such as adding a new wing to a hospital. _____

   iii. The cost of enhancing the quality of service provided by a plant asset, such as adding air conditioning. _____

   iv. The expenditure made to a plant asset that will add no benefit beyond the current accounting period. _____

   v. A repair to a plant asset that will not alter the nature of the benefit the asset provides, but will extend the assets useful life, such as adding a new roof to a building. _____

   vi. The expenditure for the initial acquisition of an asset or an additional expenditure to that plant asset that adds a benefit that extends beyond the current accounting period. _____

2. The cost of a capital expenditure is recorded as a:

   a. debit to an expense account.

   b. credit to an expense account.

   c. debit to an asset account.

   d. credit to an asset account.

3. The cost of a revenue expenditure is recorded as a:

   a. debit to an expense account.

   b. credit to an expense account.

   c. debit to an asset account.

   d. credit to a revenue account.

4. The cost of an extraordinary repair is recorded as a debit to:

   a. a repair expense account.

   b. an accumulated depreciation account.

   c. a capital account.

   d. an asset account.

5. Which of the following is true about the cost of an extraordinary repair?

   a. It increases the carrying value of the asset.

   b. It decreases the carrying value of the asset.

   c. It does not affect the carrying value of an asset.

   d. Its sole purpose is to keep the asset in good running order.

6. If a capital expenditure is incorrectly recorded as a revenue expenditure, what will be the effect on the financial statements?

   a. Net income will be overstated in the following year.

   b. Net income will be understated for the current year.

   c. Total assets will be understated at year-end.

   d. All of the above are true.

7. Christina Kaylor Architectural Renovations had purchased a machine for $25,000. It was estimated to last five years with no residual value. After three years of use, the company decided to overhaul the machine at a cost of $4,000. This overhaul would extend the life of the machine another five years beyond the original five.

   a. Prepare the journal entry to record the cost of the machine overhaul.

   b. Calculate the depreciation for the fourth year and prepare the depreciation journal entry.

8. Oreon Mann operates an outdoor center in the north Georgia mountains. Among the services he provides is outfitting rafting and canoeing expeditions with necessary equipment. Upon inspection of the outfitting equipment, Oreon decided that equipment that had been purchased for $20,000 and on which the accumulated depreciation balance was $12,000 was no longer useful. Several possible outcomes related to the disposal of the equipment are described below. Each one is independent of the other. Record each transaction in general journal form.

   a. The equipment is so badly damaged that it is left to be picked up by the waste removal service.

   b. The equipment is sold at an end-of-the-year sale of used equipment for $8,200 cash.

   c. The equipment is sold at an end-of-the-year sale of used equipment for $7,200 cash.

   d. The outfitting equipment is exchanged for office equipment with a selling price of $10,000. A trade-in allowance of $8,500 is given on the outfitting equipment. (Hint: That is a dissimilar exchange.)

   e. The outfitting equipment is exchanged for office equipment with a selling price of $10,000. A trade-in allowance of $7,200 is given on the outfitting equipment. (Hint: That is a dissimilar exchange.)

   f. The old outfitting equipment is exchanged for new outfitting equipment with a selling price of $10,000. A trade-in allowance of $8,500 is given on the old outfitting equipment. (Hint: This is a similar exchange; income tax rules are followed.)

   g. The old outfitting equipment is exchanged for new outfitting equipment with a selling price of $10,000. A trade-in allowance of $7,200 is given on the old outfitting equipment. (Hint: This is a similar exchange; income tax rules are followed.)

 Check Yourself

1. 1. (vi), 2. (iii), 3. (iv), 4. (i), 5. (v), 6. (ii) (**Additional expenditures**)

2. c. (**Additional expenditures**)

3. a. (**Additional expenditures**)

4. b. (**Additional expenditures**)

5. a. (**Additional expenditures**)

6. d. (**Additional expenditures**)

7. a.

	DR	CR
Accumulated Depreciation — Machine	4,000	
Cash		4,000

b. Original depreciation calculation:

$$\frac{\$25,000}{5 \text{ years}} = \$5,000 \text{ per year}$$

Revised carrying value:

$25,000 – (3 \times \$5,000) + \$4,000 = \$14,000$

OR

Accumulated Depreciation

Cost of overhaul	4,000	5,000	year 1
		5,000	year 2
		5,000	year 3
		11,000	balance after overhaul

Cost – Revised Accumulated Depreciation = Revised Carrying Value

$25,000 – \$11,000 = \$\underline{14,000}$

Revised depreciation calculation:

$$\frac{\$14,000}{7 \text{ years remaining}} = \$2,000 \text{ per year for years four through ten}$$

	DR	CR
Depreciation Expense — Machine	2,000	
Accumulated Depreciation — Machine		2,000

(Additional expenditures)

8.

		DR	CR
a.	Accumulated Depreciation — Outfitting Equipment	12,000	
	Loss on Disposal of Outfitting Equipment	8,000	
	Outfitting Equipment		20,000
b.	Cash	8,200	
	Accumulated Depreciation — Outfitting Equipment	12,000	
	Gain on Disposal of Outfitting Equipment		200
	Outfitting Equipment		20,000
c.	Cash	7,200	
	Accumulated Depreciation — Outfitting Equipment	12,000	
	Loss on Disposal of Outfitting Equipment	800	
	Outfitting Equipment		20,000
d.	Office Equipment	10,000	
	Accumulated Depreciation — Outfitting Equipment	12,000	
	Gain on Exchange of Outfitting Equipment		500
	Outfitting Equipment		20,000
	Cash		1,500
e.	Office Equipment	10,000	
	Accumulated Depreciation — Outfitting Equipment	12,000	
	Loss on Exchange of Outfitting Equipment	800	
	Outfitting Equipment		20,000
	Cash		2,800
f.	Outfitting Equipment (new)	9,500	
	Accumulated Depreciation — Outfitting Equipment	12,000	
	Outfitting Equipment (old)		20,000
	Cash		1,500
g.	Outfitting Equipment (new)	10,800	
	Accumulated Depreciation — Outfitting Equipment	12,000	
	Outfitting Equipment (old)		20,000
	Cash		2,800

(Disposals and exchanges)

Grade Yourself

Circle the numbers of the questions you missed, then fill in the total incorrect for each topic. If you answered more than three questions incorrectly, you need to focus on that topic. (If a topic has less than three questions and you had at least one wrong, we suggest you study that topic also. Read your textbook, a review book, or ask your teacher for help.)

Subject: Property, Plant, and Equipment: Additional Expenditures, Disposals, and Exchanges

Topic	Question Numbers	Number Incorrect
Additional expenditures	1, 2, 3, 4, 5, 6, 7	
Disposals and exchanges	8	

Other Long-Term Assets: Natural Resources and Intangible Assets

12

Brief Yourself

In this chapter we focus on two groups of long-term assets: *natural resources* and *intangible assets*. To review, consider the unique characteristics of each group, how to determine cost, and how to allocate cost. Account classifications and journal entries also must be addressed.

Natural Resources sometimes are referred to as *wasting assets*. They represent resources taken from the earth, such as minerals and timber. The cost is classified in long-term asset accounts. If land on which the natural resource is located is assigned any residual value, that cost is classified separately in the *Land* account. The cost of the natural resource must be allocated to expense over the time periods in which revenues are generated. This practice, referred to as *depletion*, is consistent with the *matching rule*. The account *Accumulated Depletion* is established as a contra-account to the Natural Resources account. This treatment is similar to that used for depreciation. The calculation to determine the amount of depletion is identical to the calculation for the *production method* of depreciation. The journal entry to record depletion is an adjusting journal entry.

	DR	CR
Depletion Expense	xx	
Accumulated Depletion		xx

Intangible Assets, in addition to being long-term assets, have the unique characteristic of having no physical properties. Intangible assets represent rights and privileges having value to a company. Patents, copyrights, trademarks, and goodwill are a few examples of intangible assets. The cost of an intangible asset also must be allocated to expense over the time period benefited. By rule, that period of time may not exceed forty years. However, if the duration of the intangible asset's legal or useful life is shorter in time than forty years, then the shorter period of time should be used as the allocation base. *Amortization* is the term used for the allocation of the intangible asset cost to expense and is recorded as an adjusting journal entry. Unlike the one for depreciation and depletion, the adjusting entry for amortization does *not* establish a contra account to the asset account. Instead, the account credited is the intangible asset account itself. Observe the example for amortization of a patent:

	DR	CR
Amortization Expense — Patent	xx	
Patent		xx

Test Yourself

1. Match each term with its corresponding definition below. Use each term only once.

   a. Wasting assets

   b. Full costing

   c. Successful efforts accounting

   d. Leasehold

   e. Patent

   f. Copyright

   g. Trademark

   h. Goodwill

   i. A legal designation, extended by the federal government for a 17-year period of time, which grants the holder the exclusive right to make a product or use a specific process. _____

   ii. The amount by which the purchase cost of a business exceeds the sum of the fair market value of the individual net assets. _____

   iii. A long-term rental agreement that gives the holder the right to occupy land and/or a facility, such as a suite of offices. _____

   iv. A method of accounting for oil and gas resources that charges the exploration costs of dry wells to a loss account deducted from the revenue of the current period. ____

   v. A term used to describe natural resources. _____

   vi. An exclusive right, if registered, to use a specific symbol to identify a product. _____

   vii. A method of accounting for oil and gas resources that capitalizes the exploration costs of dry wells. _____

   viii. An exclusive right granted by the federal government to reproduce intellectual material such as books or music for a period of time that extends 50 years beyond the death of the author. _____

2. Which of the following is not classified as a natural resource?

   a. timber tract

   b. iron ore mine

c. land

d. mineral deposits

3. The allocation of the cost of a natural resource is called:

   a. amortization expense.

   b. depreciation expense.

   c. natural resource expense.

   d. depletion expense.

4. The method to calculate depletion is identical to the calculation for which depreciation method?

   a. straight-line

   b. double-declining balance

   c. sum-of-the-years-digits

   d. production

5. If the depletion amount is different from depletion expense, it is because:

   a. the quantity of the natural resource extracted or harvested is equal to the amount sold.

   b. the quantity of the natural resource extracted or harvested is not equal to the amount sold.

   c. the allocation basis is variable.

   d. the depreciation of the drilling equipment is included in the depletion expense.

6. The cost of property, plant, and equipment closely associated with the extraction or harvesting of a natural resource should be allocated using which depreciation method?

   a. straight-line

   b. double-declining balance

   c. sum-of-the-years-digits

   d. production

7. Intangible assets are characterized by which combination of attributes?

   a. long term and no physical properties

   b. unique and no physical properties

   c. vague and unique

d. vague and no physical properties

8. The allocation of the cost of an intangible asset is called:

   a. amortization expense.

   b. depreciation expense.

   c. intangible expense.

   d. depletion expense.

9. The maximum period of time allowed by generally accepted accounting principles to amortize an intangible asset:

   a. is five years.

   b. is the shorter of its useful life, legal life, or forty years.

   c. must be written off immediately.

   d. is whatever management prefers.

10. The maximum period of time allowed by generally accepted accounting principles to carry the cost of research-and-development costs:

    a. is five years.

    b. is the shorter of its useful life, legal life, or forty years.

    c. must be written off immediately.

    d. is whatever management prefers.

11. Union Mining Company purchased a tract of land containing mineral deposits for a total cost of $1,500,000. The land was estimated to have a residual value of $100,000 upon extraction of the minerals. Mineral deposit estimates totaled 1,400,000 tons. In the first year of operation, Union Mining Company extracted and sold 300,000 tons of minerals.

    a. Record the purchase of the tract of land in general journal form.

    b. Calculate the depletion charge per ton.

    c. Calculate the depletion expense for the first year of operation.

    d. Record the depletion expense for the first year of operation.

12. Union Mining Company built dining and lodging facilities costing $60,000 for its workers. The facilities are expected to last 15 years. Union wishes to use straight-line depreciation for the facilities. Because of the remote location of the mine, the facilities will be useless after six years, when the mining operations are expected to be completed.

    Union transported mining equipment costing $140,000 to the site. Management wishes to depreciate the equipment according to the production method. The equipment will be useless upon completion of the operations at the end of the sixth year.

    a. Compute the depreciation expense for the facilities and for the equipment for Union's first year of operations at the mine.

    b. Record the depreciation in general journal form.

13. O'Neal Publishing Company purchases a copyright for an office technology textbook. The cost of the copyright is $20,000. Because of rapidly changing technology, it is expected that the textbook will be marketable for a total of fours years.

    a. Compute the amount to be amortized each year.

    b. Record the amortization expense in general journal form.

14. Dr. Dana Donaldson graduated from dental school and opened a dental practice. In order to receive affordable terms in a desirable location, she signed a ten-year lease for office space. Immediately following, she made physical improvements to the space. These included installation of new track lighting and new partitions, and renovation of the cabinetry and the bathrooms. The total cost of the improvements, which were expected to last 20 years, was $30,000.

    a. Compute the amortization of the leasehold improvements.

    b. Record the first year's amortization in general journal form.

15. Marion Company is considering the purchase of Adams Company, which has net assets valued at $300,000. Adams Company consistently generates earnings above that of the industry average of 10% of net assets. The earnings for the current year, $35,000, are representative of Adams Company's performance. Marion Company is willing to pay for goodwill up to five times the above-average earnings potential of Adams Company.

    a. Calculate the maximum amount of goodwill that Marion Company is willing to pay.

    b. Calculate the total maximum price Marion Company is willing to pay for Adams Company.

16. Olympic Resources Company purchased, for $75,000, a patent that had a remaining legal and useful life of 15 years. After five years Olympic successfully defended the patent in a lawsuit that cost $20,000.

    a. Calculate the amortization amount for each of the first five years.

    b. Record in general journal form the cost of the lawsuit.

    c. Calculate the revised annual amortization after the successful lawsuit.

Check Yourself

1. 1. (v), 2. (viii), 3. (iv), 4. (iii), 5. (i), 6. (vii), 7. (ii), 8. (vi) **(Characteristics of natural resources)**

2. c. Land is classified as property, plant, and equipment. **(Characteristics of natural resources)**

3. d. **(Depletion of natural resources)**

4. d. **(Depletion of natural resources)**

5. b. **(Depletion of natural resources)**

6. d. **(Depletion of property, plant, and equipment)**

7. a. **(Characteristics of intangible assets)**

8. a. **(Amortization of intangible assets)**

9. b. **(Amortization of intangible assets)**

10. c. **(Amortization of intangible assets)**

11. a.

	DR	CR
Land	100,000	
Natural resource	1,400,000	
Cash		1,500,000

b. $\dfrac{\$1,400,000}{1,400,000 \text{ tons}} = \$1 \text{ per ton}$

c. 300,000 tons × $1 per ton = $300,000

d.

	DR	CR
Depletion Expense	300,000	
Accumulated Depletion		300,000

(Natural resources)

12. a. Facilities

$$\frac{\$60,000}{6 \text{ years}} = \$10,000 \text{ per year}$$

Note: Use 6 years as the base, not 15, because the usefulness will expire after 6 years.

Equipment

$$\frac{300,000}{1,400,000} \times \$140,000 = \$30,000$$

Note: $\dfrac{\text{Current year productions}}{\text{Total estimated productions}} \times \text{Cost of Assets}$

b.

	DR	CR
Depreciation Expense – Facilities	10,000	
Depreciation Expense – Equipment	30,000	
Accumulated Depreciation – Facilities		10,000

(Depreciation of property, plant, and equipment closely associated with extraction of natural resources)

13. a. $\dfrac{\$20,000}{4 \text{ years}} = \$5,000 \text{ per year}$

Note: The shortest of the legal life, 40 years, and the useful life is the useful life.

b.

	DR	CR
Amortization Expense – Copyright	5,000	
Copyright		5,000

(Intangible Assets)

14. a. $\dfrac{\$30,000}{10 \text{ years}} = \$3,000 \text{ per year}$

Note: Since the duration of the lease is only 10 years, the cost of the leasehold improvements must be amortized within 10 years, not 20.

b.

	DR	CR
Amortization Expense – Leasehold Improvements	3,000	
Leasehold Improvements		3,000

(Intangible Assets)

15. a.

Adams Company earnings	$35,000	
Industry average ($300,000 x 10%)	-30,000	
Above industry average	$ 5,000	× 5 = $25,000 Goodwill

  b.

Net assets	$300,000
Goodwill	25,000
Maximum purchase price	$325,000

(Intangible Assets)

16. a. $\dfrac{\$75,000}{15 \text{ years}} = \$5,000$ patent amortization expenses per year

  b.

	DR	CR
Patent	20,000	
Cash		20,000

  c.

Purchase cost of patent	$75,000
less: 5 years amortization (5 x $5,000)	– $25,000
Balance in Patent account before lawsuit	$50,000
add: Cost of lawsuit	+ 20,000
Revised balance in Patent account	$70,000

  $70,000/10 years remaining = $7,000 revised annual amortization expense for patent

(Intangible Assets)

Grade Yourself

Circle the numbers of the questions you missed, then fill in the total incorrect for each topic. If you answered more than three questions incorrectly, you need to focus on that topic. (If a topic has less than three questions and you had at least one wrong, we suggest you study that topic also. Read your textbook, a review book, or ask your teacher for help.)

Subject: Other Long-Term Assets: Natural Resources and Intangible Assets

Topic	Question Numbers	Number Incorrect
Characteristics of natural resources	1, 2	
Depletion of natural resources	3, 4, 5	
Depletion of property, plant, and equipment	6	
Characteristics of intangible assets	7	
Amortization of intangible assets	8, 9, 10	
Natural resources	11	
Depreciation of property, plant, and equipment closely associated with extraction of natural resources	12	
Intangible assets	13, 14, 15, 16	

Partnerships

13

Brief Yourself

A partnership is a form of business organization in which two or more individuals associate to make a profit. The partnership agreement is the contract among the partners that specifies the rights and responsibilities of the partners. Although a partnership agreement may be oral, a written agreement is best for avoiding misunderstandings among partners. A partnership has unique characteristics, such as unlimited liability, limited life, and mutual agency.

Areas of emphasis when reviewing accounting for a partnership include the formation of a partnership, financial reporting of partners' capital, the sharing of partnership income and losses, admission of a new partner, retirement of a partner, and the liquidation of a partnership.

Test Yourself

1. Define a partnership.

2. Discuss the characteristics that distinguish a limited partnership from a general partnership.

3. Explain what is meant by unlimited liability.

4. What name is given to the contract among partners that defines the formation of the partnership, each partner's responsibilities, the calculation for each partner's share of the profits and losses, the terms for the admission of a new partner, the terms for withdrawal of partnership assets, the dissolution of the partnership, and the liquidation of the partnership.

5. Is it necessary for one partner to have the permission of the other partners before entering into a contract? Name the theory that supports your answer.

6. What name is used to refer to the owners' equity section of a partnership's balance sheet?

The following information pertains to Questions 7 and 8:

Ryan and Jessie each have been successful proprietors prior to deciding to form a partnership beginning May 1, 19X6. Immediately prior to the formation of the partnership, Ryan and Jessie agreed to the following information:

Assets	Ryan's Business		Jessie's Business	
	Book Value	Market Value	Book Value	Market Value
Cash	$10,000	$10,000	$5,000	$5,000
Accounts receivable (net)	11,000	9,800	7,000	6,800
Inventory	2,000	2,500	20,000	19,500
Plant assets (net)	15,000	14,200	5,000	5,200
Total assets	$38,000	$36,500	$37,000	$36,500
Liabilities and Capital				
Accounts payable	$8,800	$8,800	$2,600	$2,600
Notes payable			5,000	5,000
Ryan, Capital	29,200	27,700		
Jessie, Capital			29,400	28,900
Total liabilities and capital	$38,000	$36,500	$37,000	$36,500

7. From the information provided above, prepare the journal entry to record the formation of the partnership between Ryan and Jessie.

8. From the information provided above, prepare the new balance sheet of the Ryan and Jessie partnership immediately after its formation.

9. If the partnership agreement states that income is to be shared between Flo and Joe in a ratio of 3:2, but is silent regarding the manner in which losses are to be shared, how should losses be shared?

10. The partnership of Boris and Dianna earned $100,000 in the year 19X6. In each situation below, provide the journal entry to distribute partnership income between Boris and Dianna.

   a. No written partnership agreement exists.

   b. The written agreement indicates a 2:3 income- and loss-sharing ratio.

   c. The written agreement stipulates that income and losses are to be shared according to the average capital balances during the year, which were $50,000 for Boris and $150,000 for Dianna.

   d. The written agreement specifies that the first $30,000 of partnership income is to be allocated to Dianna for service to the partnership, and the remaining income is to be divided equally.

   e. The written agreement specifies that the first $30,000 of partnership income is to be allocated to Dianna for service to the partnership; second, that 10% interest be paid to each of the partners based on the average capital balance for the year (see *c* above); and third, that the remainder of the net income be divided equally.

   f. Repeat situation *e*, except that the net income is only $40,000.

11. What is the term used to describe the increase in capital accruing to partners upon admission of a new partner? This is the same term used to describe the additional capital accrued by a newly admitted partner in excess of the amount of tangible assets invested.

12. Nina invests $50,000 for a 40 percent interest in a partnership in which the other partners have a total capital of $100,000 immediately prior to Nina's admission. Calculate Nina's capital balance upon admission to the partnership.

13. Based on Question 12, calculate the amount of Nina's bonus.

14. Barbara and Ginny agreed to admit Louise for a 25 percent interest in their partnership in exchange for a $50,000 investment. Prior to Louise's admission, Barbara's and Ginny's capital balances were $55,000 each and they shared income and losses equally. Provide the journal entry to record Louise's admission into the partnership.

15. Based on the information in Question 14, calculate Barbara's and Ginny's new capital balances after Louise was admitted into the partnership.

16. Assuming the same facts as in Question 14, except that Louise is to be admitted for a 35 percent interest in the partnership, provide the journal entry to record the investment.

17. Based on the information in Question 16, calculate Barbara's and Ginny's new capital balances after Louise was admitted into the partnership.

18. What is the distinguishing characteristic between the dissolution of a partnership and the liquidation of a partnership?

19. Pete is retiring from the partnership of John, Al, and Pete. The books have been examined independently and the assets revalued, resulting in capital balances of $50,000, $45,000, and $40,000, respectively. John and Al have agreed to share profits and losses in a ratio of 3:2 in the new partnership. Provide journal entries to record Pete's retirement under each of the situations listed below.

   a. Pete retires and is paid cash equal to his capital balance.

   b. Pete retires, is paid $15,000 cash, and accepts a note from the partnership equal to the remainder of his capital balance.

   c. Pete retires and accepts $35,000 cash as settlement in full for his share in the partnership.

   d. John and Al agree to pay Pete $43,000 upon his retirement from the partnership.

   e. John and Al agree that Luke may be admitted to the partnership by purchasing his interest in the partnership directly from Pete. Luke pays Pete $45,000.

20. Explain the three steps necessary to liquidate a partnership.

21. Dewey, Cheatem, and Howe decided to liquidate their partnership. Their income and loss-sharing percentages were 35%, 35%, and 30%, respectively. Immediately before

		Non-cash					Capital				
Cash	+	Assets	=	Liabilities	+	Dewey	+	Cheatem	+	Howe
$6,000	+	$57,000	=	$17,000	+	$17,000	+	$15,000	+	$14,000

liquidation, they summarized their accounting equation as follows:

They sold the non-cash assets for $67,000 and completed the steps necessary to liquidate the partnership.

    a. Show the effect on the accounting equation of each step in the liquidation process.

    b. Record each step in the liquidation in general journal form.

22. Assume the same facts as in Question 21, except that the non-cash assets were sold for only $12,000. Assume the partner with the deficit paid the amount in cash to the partnership.

    a. Show the effect on the accounting equation of each step in the liquidation process.

    b. Record each step in the liquidation in general journal form.

23. Assume the same facts as in Question 21, except that the non-cash assets were sold for only $12,000. Assume the partner with the deficit did not pay the amount to the partnership. The remaining two partners absorbed the shortage.

    a. Show the effect on the accounting equation of each step in the liquidation process.

    b. Record each step in the liquidation in general journal form.

Check Yourself

1. A partnership is an association of two or more individuals engaged in a business for profit. (**Characteristics of a partnership**)

2. A limited partnership has at least one general partner and limited partners. The general partners, who run the business, have unlimited liability, and the limited partners have limited liability. (**Characteristics of a partnership**)

3. Unlimited liability refers to the potential claim that creditors of a partnership have to the personal assets of the partners if the partnership cannot pays its debts. (**Characteristics of a partnership**)

4. The partnership agreement is the contract among the partners that defines the terms of the formation of the partnership, the responsibilities of each partner, the calculation for each partner's share of the profits and losses, the terms for the admission of a new partner, the terms for withdrawal of partnership assets, the dissolution of the partnership, and the liquidation of the partnership. (**Characteristics of a partnership**)

5. It is not necessary for one partner to have the permission of the other partners before entering into a contract. The theory to support this answer is mutual agency. (**Characteristics of a partnership**)

6. The owners' equity section of a partnership's balance sheet is called Partners' Equity. (**Reporting partners' capital**)

7. The assets contributed to the new partnership are recorded on the partnership books at their market value, or at some value upon which the partners have agreed.

	DR	CR
Cash	10,000	
Accounts Receivable	9,800	
Inventory	2,500	
Plant assets	14,200	
Accounts Payable		8,800
Ryan, Capital		27,700
Cash	5,000	
Accounts Receivable	6,800	
Inventory	19,500	
Plant assets	5,200	
Accounts Payable		2,600
Notes Payable		5,000
Jessie, Capital		28,900

(**Formation of a partnership**)

8.

Ryan and Jessie Partnership
Balance Sheet
May 1, 19X6

Assets		Liabilities		
Cash	$15,000	Accounts Payable	$11,400	
Accounts Receivable	16,600	Notes Payable	5,000	
Inventory	22,000	Total Liabilities		$16,400
Plant assets (net)	19,400	Partners' Capital		
		Ryan, Capital	$27,700	
		Jessie, Capital	28,900	
		Total Partners' Capital		56,600
Total Assets	$73,000	Total Liabilities and Partners' Capital		$73,000

(Reporting partners' capital)

9. If the partnership agreement states that income is to be shared between Flo and Joe in a ratio of 3:2, but is silent regarding the manner in which losses are to be shared, losses also should be shared in a ratio of 3:2. **(Income and loss sharing among partners)**

10.

		DR	CR
a.	Income Summary	100,000	
	Boris, Capital		50,000
	Dianna, Capital		50,000
b.	Income Summary	100,000	
	Boris, Capital		40,000
	Dianna, Capital		60,000
c.	Income Summary	100,000	
	Boris, Capital		25,000
	Dianna, Capital		75,000
d.	Income Summary	100,000	
	Boris, Capital		35,000
	Dianna, Capital		65,000

10. (*continued*)

Calculation

	Boris	Dianna	Total
Service		$30,000	$30,000
Remainder	$35,000	35,000	70,000
	$35,000	$65,000	$100,000

	DR	CR
e. Income Summary	100,000	
Boris, Capital		30,000
Dianna, Capital		70,000

Calculation

	Boris	Dianna	Total
Service		$30,000	$30,000
Interest @ 10%	$5,000	15,000	20,000
Remainder	$25,000	25,000	50,000
	$30,000	$70,000	$100,000

	DR	CR
f. Income Summary	40,000	
Dianna, Capital		40,000

Calculation

	Boris	Dianna	Total
Service		$30,000	$30,000
Interest @ 10%	$5,000	15,000	20,000
Remainder	(5,000)	(5,000)	(10,000)
	$—0—	$40,000	$40,000

(Income and loss sharing among partners)

11. This additional amount of capital is called a bonus. (**Admission of a new partner**)

12. 40% ($100,000 + $50,000) = $60,000. Nina's opening capital balance will be $60,000. (**Admission of a new partner**)

13. Capital balance $60,000 – investment $50,000 = bonus $10,000. (**Admission of a new partner**)

14.

	DR	CR
Cash	50,000	
Barbara, Capital		5,000
Ginny, Capital		5,000
Louise, Capital		40,000*

*[25%($55,000 + $55,000+ $50,000) = $40,000] (**Admission of a new partner**)

15. Barbara: $55,000 + $5,000 = $60,000; Ginny: $55,000 + $5,000 = $60,000 (**Admission of a new partner**)

16.

	DR	CR
Cash	50,000	
Barbara, Capital	3,000	
Ginny, Capital	3,000	
Louise, Capital		56,000*

*[35%($50,000 + 55,000 + $50,000) = $56,000] (**Admission of a new partner**)

17. Barbara: $55,000 – $3,000 = $52,000
Ginny: $55,000 – $3,000 = $52,000 (**Admission of a new partner**)

18. The distinguishing characteristic between the dissolution of a partnership and the liquidation of a partnership is that the business of the partnership may continue after a dissolution, but will not continue after a liquidation. (**Dissolution of a partnership**)

19.

		DR	CR
a.	Pete, Capital	40,000	
	Cash		40,000
b.	Pete, Capital	40,000	
	Cash		15,000
	Note Payable		25,000
c.	Pete, Capital	40,000	
	Cash		35,000
	John, Capital		3,000
	Al, Capital		2,000
d.	Pete, Capital	40,000	
	John, Capital	1,800	
	Al, Capital	1,200	
	Cash		43,000
e.	Pete, Capital	40,000	
	Luke, Capital		40,000

(*Hint:* The partnership did not receive the $45,000 cash from Luke.)
(Dissolution of a partnership)

20. The three steps necessary to liquidate a partnership include: 1) sale of the partnership's non-cash assets, with the gain or loss from the sale shared by the partners in their income- and loss-sharing ratio; 2) payment of liabilities to outside creditors of the partnership; 3) distribution of remaining cash to the partners according to their capital balances. **(Liquidation of a partnership)**

21. a.

		Cash	+	Non-cash Assets	=	Liabilities	+	Dewey	Capital Cheatem	Howe
		$6,000	+	$57,000	=	$17,000	+	$17,000	$15,000	$14,000
		+ 67,000	+	- 57,000				+ 3,500	+ $35,000	+ 3,000
		$73,000	+	—0—	=	$17,000	+	$20,500	$18,500	$17,000
		- 17,000				- 17,000		20,500	$18,500	$17,000
		$56,000	+	—0—	=	—0—	+	$20,500	$18,500	$17,000
		- 56,000	+					- 20,500	$18,500	- 17,000
		—0—	+	—0—	=	—0—	+	—0—	—0—	—0—

b.

	DR	CR
Cash	67,000	
Non-cash Assets		57,000
Dewey, Capital		3,500
Cheatem, Capital		3,500
Howe, Capital		3,010
Liabilities	17,000	
Cash		17,000
Dewey, Capital	20,500	
Cheatem, Capital	18,500	
Howe, Capital	17,000	
Cash		56,000

(Liquidation of a partnership)

22. a.

	Cash	+	Non-cash Assets	=	Liabilities	+	Dewey	Capital Cheatem	Howe
	$6,000	+	$57,000	=	$17,000	+	$17,000	$15,000	$14,000
	+ 12,000		− 57,000				− 15,750	− 15,750	− 13,500
	$18,000	+	—0—	=	$17,000	+	$1,250	$(750)	$500
	− 17,000				− 17,000				
	$1,000	+	—0—	=	—0—	+	$1,250	$(750)	$500
	+ 750							+ 750	
	$1,750		—0—	=	—0—	+	$1,250	—0—	$500
	− 1,750						− 1,250		− 500
	—0—	+	—0—	=	—0—	+	—0—	—0—	—0—

b.

	DR	CR
Cash	12,000	
Dewey, Capital	15,750	
Cheatem, Capital	15,750	
Howe, Capital	13,500	
Non-cash Assets		57,000
Liabilities	17,000	
Cash		17,000
Cash	750	
Cheatem, Capital		750
Dewey, Capital	1,250	
Howe, Capital	500	
Cash		1,750

(Liquidation of a partnership)

23. a.

Cash	+	Non-cash Assets	=	Liabilities	+	Dewey	Capital Cheatem	Howe
$6,000	+	$57,000	=	$17,000	+	$17,000	$15,000	$14,000
+ 12,000	+	– 57,000				– 15,750	– 15,750	– 13,500
$18,000		—0—	=	$17,000	+	$1,250	$(750)	$500
– 17,000			=	– 17,000				
$1,000	+	—0—	=	—0—	+	$1,250	$(750)	$500
						– 405	+ 750	– 345*
$1,000		—0—	=	—0—	+	$845	—0—	$155
						– 845		– 155
– 1,000	+							
—0—	+	—0—	=	—0—	+	—0—	—0—	—0—

*35% (Dewey) + 30% (Howe) = 65% (total)
35 (Dewey)/65 (total) = 54% (Dewey's share of deficit) 0.54 x $750 deficit = $405
30 (Howe)/65 (total) = 46% (Howe's share of deficit) 0.46 x $750 deficit = $345

b.

	DR	CR
Cash	12,000	
Dewey, Capital	15,750	
Cheatem, Capital	15,750	
Howe, Capital	13,500	
Non-cash Assets		57,000
Liabilities	17,000	
Cash		17,000
Dewey, Capital	405	
Howe, Capital	345	
Cheatem, Capital		750
Dewey, Capital	845	
Howe, Capital	155	
Cash		1,000

(Liquidation of a partnership)

Grade Yourself

Circle the numbers of the questions you missed, then fill in the total incorrect for each topic. If you answered more than three questions incorrectly, you need to focus on that topic. (If a topic has less than three questions and you had at least one wrong, we suggest you study that topic also. Read your textbook, a review book, or ask your teacher for help.)

Subject: Partnerships

Topic	Question Numbers	Number Incorrect
Characteristics of a partnership	1, 2, 3, 4, 5	
Reporting partners' capital	6, 8	
Formation of a partnership	7	
Income and loss sharing among partners	9, 10	
Admission of a new partner	11, 12, 13, 14, 15, 16, 17	
Dissolution of a partnership	18, 19	
Liquidation of a partnership	20, 21, 22, 23	

Corporations: Contributed Capital

14

 ## Brief Yourself

In this chapter our attention turns to financial accounting for the corporation. To prepare for this chapter, review first the characteristics of corporations, including the advantages and disadvantages of the corporate form of business, the rights and privileges of stockholders, and the nature of dividends. Next, review an example of a stockholders' equity section of a corporate balance sheet, noting the divisions and the account titles. Review also journal entries that establish and maintain those accounts—for example, the issuance of capital stock.

The organizers of a corporation apply to a state for authorization to operate. They do this by submitting the *articles of incorporation*, which provide all the important information about the corporation. When the state approves the application, it grants the corporation a *charter* to operate. The organizers of the new corporation solicit investors.

These investors become owners of the company. They are referred to as *stockholders*. Their level of *ownership* and *voting power* is measured by the number of their *shares of stock*. The stockholders elect the *board of directors*, which establishes the *major policies* of the corporation. The board of directors chooses the *management team*, which *implements* or *executes* those policies.

The corporation has become the predominant form of business in the United States. Historically, as businesses required more capital, the corporate structure became an attractive vehicle to meet this objective. A large number of potential investors (*ease of generating capital*) could be involved and would be offered *limited liability*. These two are among the advantages listed in most texts. In most texts limited liability is also listed as a disadvantage.

Organization costs are those costs that a corporation incurs initially and are necessary for its existence. Examples include the fees from attorneys and accountants, as well as the fee to the secretary of state's office for the issuance of the charter. Sometimes the attorneys and accountants are willing to be paid in stock instead of cash. This is an example of a *non-cash transaction*. The secretary of state, however, is always paid in cash.

Organization costs are classified on the balance sheet as an *intangible asset. Amortization expense-organization costs* is reported on the income statement with the operating expenses. The amount of amortization is usually calculated on a straight-line basis using five years as a base (denominator).

The *stockholders' equity section* of a corporate balance sheet has two major divisions: *contributed capital*, and *retained earnings*. Some companies refer to contributed capital as *paid-in capital*. The choice of terms is a matter of preference. The contributed capital section lists all the elements of the corporation's capital that has been paid in by investors, such as the stock accounts. The retained earnings section refers to the earnings generated by the corporation from its very beginning that have not been paid out in dividends or offset by any losses. Were the corporation ever to liquidate, the stockholders would have a claim to the contributed capital and to the retained earnings.

Cash dividends are the distribution of some of the earnings of the corporation to the stockholders. Cash dividends must be declared by the *board of directors*. Auditors frequently check the minutes of the meeting of the board of directors to see if the will of the board of directors has been executed.

The important dates regarding cash dividends are:

1) date of declaration;

2) date of record;

3) date of payment.

On the *date of declaration* the board of directors makes public its intention to pay dividends in the form of cash to the stockholders. This announcement creates a current liability. The journal entry on that date reflects the creation of a liability. No journal entry is prepared on the *date of record*. This date is important because it creates a cutoff to determine which stockholders receive the dividends and which do not in instances when the stock is sold sometime between the date of declaration and the date of payment. The *date of payment* is important because the corporation pays its stockholders their dividends in the form of cash. The journal entry reflects the liability being canceled and the cash being reduced.

If two classes of stockholders exist, it is important to calculate correctly the allocation of dividends between the two groups. When the dividends on the preferred stock are *cumulative*, the following steps lead to the necessary allocation:

Steps for dividend allocation:

1) Determine how much in dividends the preferred stockholders should receive. That formula is: the number of preferred shares outstanding multiplied by the par value of the preferred multiplied by the percentage given before the par value.

2) Determine how many years, if any, the dividends are in arrears. Your answer from Step 1 is multiplied by the number of years. The result is the amount of dividends to be distributed to the preferred shareholders. Of course, if the available dividends are less than the amount to which the preferred are entitled, your answer is limited by whatever amount is available. Any amount due but not paid because of a shortage is carried over to the following year. That becomes the new amount in arrears.

3) To determine the amount of dividends to be paid to the common stockholders, deduct from total available dividends whatever amount has been allocated to the preferred stockholders. Whatever amount remains goes to the common stockholders. Sometimes no dividends remain for the common stockholders.

If the preferred stock is *non-cumulative*, then dividends in arrears is *not* an issue. In any one year the preferred dividends are never more than the amount calculated in Step 1, and whatever amount remains goes to the common stockholders.

Test Yourself

1. Match each term with its corresponding definition below. Use each term only once.

   a. Ex-dividend

   b. Issued stock

   c. Authorized shares

   d. Callable preferred stock

   e. Stock certificate

   f. Stock option

   g. Par value

   h. Dividend in arrears

   i. Organization costs

   j. Proxy

   k. Premium

   l. Discount

   i. A document conveying ownership of a specified number of shares of stock. _____

   ii. A per-share dollar amount assigned to shares of stock within a class of stock; used to calculate the minimum legal capital. _____

   iii. Unpaid dividends owed on cumulative preferred stock. _____

   iv. An attribute of capital stock during the time between the date of record and the date of payment of the dividend; significant because the right to receive a dividend payment does not transfer to the party purchasing the stock during this period of time. _____

   v. Shares of stock that at one time have been transferred to stockholders; may include shares temporarily held in the treasury of the corporation. _____

   vi. Preferred stock that may be redeemed and retired at the option of the corporation. _____

   vii. A right to purchase stock at a predetermined price; usually granted to employees of a corporation. _____

   viii. Costs, such as legal and incorporation fees incurred, that are necessary in the formation of a corporation. _____

   ix. A legal transfer of votes attached to shares of stock by a stockholder to another party. _____

   x. The maximum number of shares of stock permitted by a corporate charter granted by a state; includes potential shares and issued shares. _____

   xi. An alternate name used by corporations to report the amount in excess of par value paid by investors for stock . _____

   xii. A name used by corporations to report the amount less than par value paid by investors for stock (permitted only in some states). _____

2. The application for obtaining a state charter is called the:

   a. corporate papers.

   b. articles of incorporation.

   c. articles of organization.

   d. organization papers.

3. Which of the following attributes is least likely associated with preferred stock?

   a. voting

   b. callable

   c. convertible

   d. cumulative

4. Which of the following is *not* among the advantages of the corporate form of business?

   a. ease of raising capital

   b. separate legal entity

   c. unlimited liability

   d. professional management

5. Which of the following generally is viewed as an advantage of the corporate form of business, but may be regarded as a disadvantage in some situations?

   a. ease of raising capital

   b. separate legal entity

   c. limited liability

   d. professional management

6. Which group defines corporate policy?

   a. stockholders

   b. underwriters

   c. managers

   d. board of directors

7. If stock without par value (no-par stock) has a stated value, the excess of the issued amount over

the stated value should be credited to the account as:

   a. Paid-in Capital in Excess of Par Value, Common.

   b. Paid-in Capital in Excess of Stated Value, Common.

   c. Common Stock.

   d. Revenue.

8. A contract between a corporation and investors who agree to purchase corporate stock at an agreed price through installment payments is known as a:

   a. stock advance.

   b. stock layaway.

   c. stock subscription.

   d. stock prospectus.

9. Sawyer Corporation is authorized to issue 10,000 shares of 6%, $50 par value preferred stock and 150,000 shares of $4 par value common stock. On March 1, 19X5, Sawyer issues 100 shares of preferred stock at $51 per share and 1,000 shares of common stock at $6 per share. Record the issuance of the stock in general journal form.

10. On December 1, 19X5, Sawyer Corporation declares dividends of $15,300 to stockholders of record on December 20, to be paid January 31, 19X6. On December 31, 19X5, after revenue and expense accounts had been closed, Sawyer Corporation's Income Summary account had a credit balance of $25,000. Record all necessary journal entries pertaining to dividends, including closing entries.

11. Referring to the information contained in Questions 9 and 10:

    a. calculate the December 31, 19X5, balance in the Retained Earnings account.

    b. prepare the Liabilities section and the Stockholders' Equity section of Sawyer.

12. Sierra Products, Inc., has 20,000 shares 8% $100 par cumulative preferred stock and 50,000 shares $5 par common stock outstanding. Total cash dividends paid for each of 4 years are:

Year	Dividends
1	—0—
2	$125,000
3	225,000
4	325,000

    a. Calculate the allocation of the cash dividends to each class of stockholders in total and on a per share basis.

    b. Repeat (a) assuming the preferred stock is noncumulative.

13. Record in general journal form the transactions of Newcom Company, a brand-new company.

    a. Paid $100 to the state for a corporate charter.

    b. Negotiated with legal counsel an exchange of 100 shares of its $10 par common stock for services necessary to incorporate. The attorney's services normally would be billed at $1,400.

    c. Negotiated with its newly selected CPA an exchange of 150 shares of its $10 par common stock for accounting and tax services necessary to incorporate. The CPA's services normally would be billed at $2,250.

    d. At the end of the first year of operation, Newcom Company makes an adjusting entry for the amortization of the Organization Costs. It decides to use a five year straight line basis.

14. Bashor Company negotiated a contract with investors for a stock subscription. Following an initial down payment of 25% of the total, the remainder would be paid in three equal installments at the end of each quarter for three quarters. The subscription price of the $8 par common stock was $10 per share for all 80,000 shares in the subscription. Record the transactions in general journal form.

    a. The establishment of the subscription, including the down payment.

    b. The receipt of the first installment one quarter later.

    c. The early receipt in full of the amount due from investors holding one-half of the subscriptions.

    d. The receipt of the second installment from the remaining investors holding subscriptions.

    e. The receipt of the third installment from the remaining investors holding subscriptions.

15. Referring to the information in Question 14, prepare the stockholders' equity section of the balance sheet immediately after completion of transaction (*c*).

Check Yourself

1. 1. (v), 2. (vii), 3. (viii), 4. (i), 5. (ii), 6. (iv), 7. (vi), 8. (ix), 9. (x), 10. (iii), 11. (xi), 12. (i)
    (Characteristics of corporations)

2. b. **(Characteristics of corporations)**

3. a. **(Characteristics of corporations)**

4. c. *Limited* liability is an advantage of a corporation. **(Characteristics of corporations)**

5. c. **(Characteristics of corporations)**

6. d. **(Characteristics of corporations)**

7. b. **(Characteristics of corporations)**

8. c. **(Characteristics of corporations)**

9.

			DR	CR
March	1	Cash	11,100	
		Preferred Stock		5,000
		Premium on Preferred Stock		100
		Common Stock		4,000
		Premium on Common Stock		2,000

(Recording instance of stock for cash)

10.

			DR	CR
December	1	Cash Dividends Declared	15,300	
		Cash Dividends Payable		15,300
December	20	No entry		
December	31	Income Summary	25,000	
		Retained Earnings		25,000
December	31	Retained Earnings	15,300	
		Cash Dividend Declared		15,300
January	31	Cash Dividends Payable	15,300	
		Cash		15,300

(Recording the declaration and payment of cash dividends, and the closing of dividends declared and income summary)

11. a.

Retained Earnings

Closed cash dividend declared	15,300	–0–	Beginning balance
		25,000	Dec. 31, closed income summary
		9,700	Ending Balance

b.

Sawyer Corporation
Balance Sheet (partial)
December 31, 19X5

Liabilities

Current Liabilities:

Cash Dividends Payable		15,300

Stockholders' Equity

Paid-in Capital:

Preferred Stock	$5,000		
Premium on Preferred Stock	100	$5,100	
Common Stock	$4,000		
Premium on Common Stock	2,000	6,000	
Total Paid-in Capital		$11,100	
Retained Earnings		9,700	
Total Stockholders' Equity			20,800
Total Liabilities and Stockholders' Equity			$36,100

(Preparing the liabilities and stockholders' equity sections of the corporate balance sheet)

12. Annual dividend for preferred stock: 20,000 × $100 × 8% = $160,000.

a.

Year	Total Dividends	Preferred Dividends	Preferred Per Share	Common Dividends	Common Per Share
1	—0—	—0—	—0—	—0—	—0—
2	$125,000	$125,000	$6.25	—0—	—0—
3	225,000	225,000	11.25	—0—	—0—
4	325,000	290,000	14.50	$35,000	$0.70

b.

Year	Total Dividends	Preferred Dividends	Preferred Per Share	Common Dividends	Common Per Share
1	—0—	—0—	—0—	—0—	—0—
2	$125,000	$125,000	$6.25	—0—	—0—
3	225,000	160,000	8.00	$65,000	$1.30
4	325,000	160,000	8.00	$165,000	3.30

(Allocation for cash dividends between preferred and common stock)

13.

		DR	CR
a.	Organization Costs	100	
	Cash		100
b.	Organization Costs	1,400	
	Common Stock		1,000
	Premium on Common Stock		400
c.	Organization Costs	2,250	
	Common Stock		1,500
	Premium on Common Stock		750
d.	Amortization Expense — Organization Costs	750*	
	Organization Costs		750

$$*[\frac{100 + 1,400 + 2,250}{5} = 750]$$ **(Accounting for organization costs)**

14.

		DR	CR
a.	Cash	200,000	
	Subscriptions Receivable	600,000	
	Common Stock Subscribed		640,000
	Premium on Common Stock		160,000
b.	Cash	200,000	
	Subscriptions Receivable		200,000
c.	Cash	200,000	
	Subscriptions Receivable		200,000
	Common Stock Subscribed	320,000	
	Common Stock		320,000
d.	Cash	100,000	
	Subscriptions Receivable		100,000
e.	Cash	100,000	
	Subscriptions Receivable		100,000
	Common Stock Subscribed	320,000	
	Common Stock		320,000

(Accounting for stock subscriptions)

15.

Bashor Company
Balance Sheet [partial]
Date

Stockholders' Equity	
Paid-in Capital:	
Common Stock ($8 par, 40,000 shares outstanding)	$320,000
Common Stock Subscribed	320,000
Premium on Common Stock	160,000
Total Paid in Capital	$800,000

(Accounting for stock subscriptions)

Grade Yourself

Circle the numbers of the questions you missed, then fill in the total incorrect for each topic. If you answered more than three questions incorrectly, you need to focus on that topic. (If a topic has less than three questions and you had at least one wrong, we suggest you study that topic also. Read your textbook, a review book, or ask your teacher for help.)

Subject: Corporations: Contributed Capital

Topic	Question Numbers	Number Incorrect
Characteristics of corporations	1, 2, 3, 4, 5, 6, 7, 8	
Recording issuance of stock for cash	9	
Recording the declaration and payment of cash dividends, and the closing of dividends declared and income summary	10	
Preparing the liabilities and stockholders' equity sections of the corporate balance sheet	11	
Allocation for cash dividends between preferred and common stock	12	
Accounting for organization costs	13	
Accounting for stock subscriptions	14, 15	

Corporations: Retained Earnings and Income Statement

15

Brief Yourself

This chapter continues the examination of corporate stockholders' equity, with an emphasis on the retained earnings section. Topics include stock dividends, stock splits, treasury stock, the retained earnings statement, the restriction of retained earnings, and book value. This chapter also examines the corporate income statement and earnings per share.

The balance in the *retained earnings* account represents the profits of a company from its very beginning less any losses and any distribution of dividends. It is important to study and note which activities will *change the retained earnings balance*.

A *prior period adjustment* is a *correction of an accounting error* made in a year before the current year. A prior period adjustment should be reported as a separate line item after the opening balance on the retained earnings statement. It should be reported net of its tax effect. A prior period adjustment will result in an adjustment (increase or decrease) to the beginning balance of retained earnings. An adjusting journal entry is also made to increase or decrease the retained earnings account balance in the general ledger.

A *credit balance* in Income Summary is closed with a debit to Income Summary and a *credit to retained earnings*. This results in an increase to retained earnings.

A *debit balance* in Income Summary is closed with a *debit to retained earnings* (a decrease) and a credit to Income Summary.

The *Cash Dividends Declared* account is closed with a credit, and then a *debit to retained earnings* (a decrease).

The amount of a *stock dividend* is transferred to the contributed capital accounts with credits. The *retained earnings account is debited* (a decrease).

A *small stock dividend* is a distribution of additional shares of stock equal to *no more than 20%-25%* of the outstanding shares of stock. A *large stock dividend* is a distribution of additional shares of stock that amounts to *more than 20% to 25%* of the outstanding shares.

The amount of a small stock dividend is calculated as follows:

# of outstanding shares of stock × % (given) of stock dividend × market value of stock

The amount of a small stock dividend is debited to retained earnings. The credit side of the entry is divided between two accounts. Using the same calculation as above, but substituting *par* value for market value, will give the credit to *Common Stock Distributable.* This account is temporary, and eventually will be closed to common stock when the shares are issued. The other credit is made to *Paid-in Capital in Excess of Par Value—Common.* The amount credited to that account is determined by using the same calculation again, but instead of market value, substituting the difference between market and par, the excess.

A stock dividend, small or large, is a transfer from retained earnings to contributed capital. Thus, retained earnings decreases while contributed capital increases. *Total stockholders' equity does not change as a result of a stock dividend.*

A large stock dividend is calculated by using par value, not market value. Since market value is ignored, no excess exists. Retained Earnings is debited, and a credit is made to common stock distributable.

A *stock split* occurs when a corporation wishes to force down the market price of its stock. This usually occurs with very successful companies whose stock prices have skyrocketed, making them out of reach of the average investor. By diluting the market with additional shares, the market price will decrease, at least at first. This affords more investors participation in trading that stock. In theory, the stockholder does not benefit from a split. For instance:

before stock split:	100 shares × $8 par = $800 total book value
after stock split:	200 shares × $4 par = $800 total book value

In practice, a split is usually very advantageous to the original stockholders. Although the new market value is diluted at first, it begins to spiral upward again. The investor, now having twice or three times the shares held before, has been enhanced.

A stock split does not change contributed capital and it does not change retained earnings. No journal entry is made for a stock split.

Treasury stock is stock that already has been issued and is bought back by the company. There are a number of reasons why they may take this action. One is to have stock available to reissue to employees in stock option plans.

Treasury stock is accounted for at cost. Just debit treasury stock and credit cash.

In the balance sheet, treasury stock is reported as the last item in stockholders' equity. It is deducted from the total of contributed capital and retained earnings to arrive at total stockholders' equity.

Treasury stock is a *contra-stockholders' equity account.* As with all contra-accounts, it has a balance opposite from the accounts to which it is related, and so must be deducted from the balances of those accounts. The treasury stock account has a debit balance, whereas the usual stockholders' equity accounts have credit balances. A *common mistake* is to think of treasury stock as an asset because it has a debit balance.

Retained earnings is restricted by the board of directors to let stockholders know that not all the retained earnings are available for payment in dividends. A *restriction of retained earnings* does not physically set aside assets in a fund. To make that happen, another transaction specifically transferring assets must occur.

A restriction of retained earnings occurs for one of three general reasons: 1) voluntarily; 2) contractual agreement; and 3) state law. A voluntary restriction might occur because a company is planning a plant expansion. A contractual agreement may provide for a restriction to protect the creditor. State law may require a restriction if a company holds treasury stock.

Total retained earnings is not affected by a restriction, nor is total stockholders' equity. A restriction of retained earnings is reported on the balance sheet as a *separate line item* in the retained earnings section of stockholders' equity. Usually, the *notes to the financial statements* includes a reference to the restriction.

Book value, not to be confused with par or market value, is a calculation necessary in certain instances. It may be beneficial to review some concepts before examining this topic. Sometimes the stockholders' equity is referred to as the *net assets* of the corporation. This term relates to the basic *accounting equation.* Remember: Assets = Liabilities + Owner's Equity. Now our owners are stockholders, so Assets = Liabilities + *Stockholders' Equity.* Rearranging this equation results in the equation Assets – Liabilities = Stockholders' Equity. Starting with the total assets of a corporation and deducting the liabilities, which are really the claims from outsiders, leaves the claims of the stockholders, or the net assets.

If no preferred stock exists, then book value per share =

$$\frac{total\ stockholders'\ equity}{\#\ of\ shares\ of\ stock\ outstanding}$$

If preferred stock exists, then book value per share is calculated in steps. Begin with:

1) Total stockholders' equity

2) *less* Preferred Stockholders' portion (dividends in arrears and the call price or par value of the preferred stock)

3) = Common Stockholders' portion

4) $\dfrac{Common\ Stockholders'\ portion}{\#\ of\ common\ shares\ outstanding}$ = *Book value per common share*

As noted above, corporate net income is a component of retained earnings, and, accordingly, most texts include the corporate income statement and earnings per share with the study of retained earnings. The very nature of corporate business requires that the corporate income statement contain categories not used on income statements of a sole proprietorship or of a partnership. The first major difference observed on a corporate income statement is the line item for income tax expense. Other possible differences include gains or losses from discontinued operations, extraordinary gains or losses, and income or losses from the cumulative effect of an accounting change. Each of the latter three is reported net of taxes.

It is customary to report earnings per share information below the main body of the corporate income statement. *Simple earnings per share* is computed by the following equation:

$$\frac{net\ income\ available\ to\ common\ stockholders}{number\ of\ shares\ of\ common\ stock\ outstanding}$$

Test Yourself

1. Retained Earnings is best described as:

   a. excess cash after completing operations for the current year.

   b. net income of the current year less dividends paid.

   c. the accumulated profits of the company from its first year of operations through the present, reduced by dividends and losses.

   d. cash saved for special projects.

2. Which of the following statements is true about an appropriation of retained earnings?

   a. It sets aside cash for the special purpose of the appropriation.

   b. It increases total retained earnings by the amount of the appropriation.

   c. It increases total stockholders' equity by the amount of the appropriation.

   d. It shifts a portion of retained earnings into a restricted account to convey the message that some of retained earnings is not available for dividend payments.

3. Which pair is the correct combination to describe the effect of an appropriation of retained earnings on total retained earnings and total stockholders' equity, respectively?

	Total Retained Earnings	Total Stockholders' Equity
a.	No effect	No effect
b.	Increase	No effect
c.	No effect	Increase
d.	Increase	Decrease

4. Which of the following is reported on a statement of retained earnings?

   a. extraordinary items

   b. cumulative effect of an accounting change

   c. discontinued operations

   d. prior period adjustments

5. Which pair is the correct combination to describe the effect of a stock dividend on total retained earnings and total stockholders' equity, respectively?

	Total Retained Earnings	Total Stockholders' Equity
a.	Increase	Decrease
b.	Decrease	No effect
c.	Decrease	Increase
d.	Decrease	Decrease

6. The dollar amount of a 10% stock dividend is calculated by multiplying 10% times:

a. the number of authorized shares times the par value of the stock.

b. the number of outstanding shares time the par value of the stock.

c. the number of outstanding shares times the market value of the stock on the day of declaration.

d. the number of outstanding shares times the market value of the stock on the day of distribution.

7. Which pair is the correct combination to describe the effect of a stock split on total contributed capital and par value per share, respectively?

	Total Contributed Capital	Par Value Per Share
a.	Increase	Decrease
b.	Increase	No effect
c.	No effect	Decrease
d.	No effect	No effect

8. Which of the following situations requires a prior period adjustment?

a. the loss from earthquake damage

b. the loss from decline in inventory values

c. the reversal of depreciation expense taken on land in past years

d. the effect of shifting from FIFO inventory to LIFO inventory

9. The purchase by a company of its own stock is identified as:

a. treasury stock.

b. preferred stock.

c. subscribed stock.

d. distributable stock.

10. What is the most probable explanation about a company which has issued 50,000 shares of common stock and has 45,000 shares outstanding?

a. The company issued the shares at less than par value.

b. The company is holding 5,000 shares in the treasury.

c. The company declared a 10% stock dividend.

d. The loss in earnings was $5,000.

11. Which of the following is accurate about the statement of stockholders' equity?

a. It is a condensed version of the stockholders' equity section of the balance sheet.

b. It reports the dividends payable at the end of the year.

c. It reports the operations discontinued during the year.

d. It reports the changes in the stockholders' equity accounts during the year.

12. Palermo, Inc., which has 50,000 shares of $6 par value stock outstanding, declared a 5% stock dividend on July 1, 19X5, for stockholders of record on July 16, to be distributed on August 1. The market value of the Palermo stock on July 1 was $20. On August 15, Palermo declared a ten-cents-per-share cash dividend. Record the above events and the closing entries for the dividend transactions in general journal form.

13. Referring to Question 12, prepare a partial stockholders' equity section of the Palermo, Inc., balance sheet for July 31, 19X5. Prior to July 1, the Paid-in Capital in Excess of Par Value, Common account and the Retained Earnings account balances had been $100,000 and $500,000, respectively.

14. Adams, Inc., which has 75,000 shares of $4 par value common stock issued and outstanding, purchased 10,000 shares of its own stock for $12 per share on January 20, 19X6. On February 20, Adams sold 2,000 shares for $14 per share. On March 20, Adams sold 5,000 shares for $11 per share. Adams, Inc. had had no prior treasury stock transactions. Record the above transactions in general journal form.

15. Referring to the information in Question 14, prepare the stockholders' equity section of Adams, Inc.'s March 31, 19X6 balance sheet. Additional stockholders' equity information for Adams, Inc., on March 31: Paid-in Capital in Excess of Par Value, Common, $75,000, and Retained Earnings, $225,000.

16. Németh Industries, Inc., a closely held corporation, would like to determine the book values per share of both its preferred stock and its common stock. The following December 31, 19X5, stockholders' equity information is available:

Preferred Stock* ($100 par, 6% cumulative, 10,000 shares issued and outstanding)	$1,000,000
Common Stock ($3 par, 100,000 shares issued, 97,000 shares outstanding)	300,000
Paid-in Capital in Excess of PAV on Common Stock	50,000
Retained Earnings	235,000
Treasury Stock	30,000

*The preferred stock is callable at $102; the dividends on the preferred stock are one year in arrears.

17. A partial list of general ledger balances of Mihály Company on December 31, before closing entries, appears below.

Account Name	Balance
Preferred stock, 8%, $100 par, 800 shares issued	$80,000
Common stock, $5 par, 30,000 shares issued	150,000
Retained earnings, beginning, unadjusted	98,000
Dividends	14,000
Sales revenue	640,000
Cost of goods sold	390,000
Selling expenses	72,000
General expenses	67,000
Gain on sale of equipment	20,000
Interest expense	15,000
Income tax expense on continuing operations	34,000
Income from discontinued operations	26,000
Income tax expense on income from discontinued operations	8,000
Loss from sale of discontinued operations	13,000
Tax savings on loss from sale of discontinued operations	4,000
Extraordinary gain	22,000
Income tax expense on extraordinary gain	7,000

Prepare a multistep income statement with the earnings per share presentation included and a statement of retained earnings. No changes occurred in the stock account balances during the year. A prior period adjustment resulting in a $10,000 credit to retained earnings will be recorded.

Check Yourself

1. c. **(Retained earnings)**

2. d. **(Retained earnings)**

3. a. **(Retained earnings)**

4. d. **(Retained earning)**

5. b. **(Stock dividends)**

6. c. **(Stock dividends)**

7. c. **(Stock split)**

8. c. **(Fire period adjustment)**

9. a. **(Treasury stock)**

10. b. **(Treasury stock)**

11. d. **(Statement of stockholders' equity)**

12.

				DR	CR
July	1	Stock Dividend Declared		50,000	
		(50,000 × 5% × $20)			
		Common Stock Distributable			15,000
		(50,000 × 5% × $6)			
		Paid-in Capital in Excess of Par Value, Common			35,000
		[50,000 × 5% × ($20 – $6)]			
July	16	no entry			
July	31	Retained Earnings		50,000	
		Stock Dividend Declared			50,000
August	1	Common Stock Distributable		15,000	
		Common Stock			15,000
August	15	Cash Dividend Declared		5,250	
		(50,000 × 1.05 × $0.10)			
		Cash Dividend Payable			5,250
August	31	Retained Earnings		5,250	
		Cash Dividend Declared			5,250

(Stock dividends)

13.

Palermo, Inc.
Balance Sheet [partial]
July 31, 19X5

Stockholders' Equity	
Contributed Capital:	
Common Stock (50,000 shares issued and outstanding, $6 par)	$300,000
Common Stock Distributable (2,500 shares)	15,000
Paid-in Capital in Excess of Par Value, Common	135,000
Total Contributed Capital	$450,000
Retained Earnings	450,000
Total Stockholders' Equity	$900,000

Retained Earnings				Paid-in Capital in Excess of Par, Common		
July 31	50,000	50,000	Beginning Balance		100,000	Beginning Balance
		450,000			35,000	July 1
					135,000	

(Stock dividends)

14.

				DR	CR
January	20	Treasury Stock [(10,000 × $12)]		120,000	
		Cash			120,000
February	20	Cash [(2,000 × $14)]		28,000	
		Treasury Stock [(2,000 × $12)]			24,000
		Paid-in Capital, Treasury Stock [2,000 × ($14 – $12)]			4,000
March	20	Cash [(5,000 × $11)]		55,000	
		Paid-in Capital, Treasury Stock		4,000*	
		Retained Earnings		1,000	
		Treasury Stock [(5,000 × $12)]			60,000

*The Paid-in Capital, Treasury Stock account cannot be debited for more than its credit balance. In other words, it cannot have a debit balance. **(Treasury stock)**

15.

Adams, Inc.
Balance Sheet [partial]
March 31, 19X6

Stockholders' Equity

Contributed Capital:	
Common Stock ($4 par, 75,000 shares issued, 72,000 shares outstanding)	$300,000
Paid-in Capital in Excess of Par Value, Common	75,000
Total Contributed Capital	$375,000
Retained Earnings	224,000
Total Contributed Capital and Retained Earnings	$599,000
Less: Treasury Stock (at cost)	36,000
Total Stockholders' Equity	$563,000

Treasury Stock			Retained Earnings		
Jan. 20	120,000	50,000 Feb. 20	Mar. 20 1,000	225,000 Beginning Balance	
		60,000 Mar. 20		224,000	
	36,000				

(Treasury stock)

16.

Németh Industries, Inc.
Balance Sheet [partial]
December 31, 19X5

Preferred Stock ($100 par, 6% cumulative, 10,000 shares issued and outstanding)	$1,000,000	
Common Stock ($3 par, 100,000 shares issued, 97,000 shares outstanding)	300,000	
Premium on Common Stock	50,000	
Total Contributed Capital	$1,350,000	
Retained Earnings	235,000	
Total Contributed Capital and Retained Earnings	$1,585,000	
Less: Treasury Stock	30,000	
Total Stockholders' Equity	$1,555,000	
Total Stockholders' Equity		$1,555,000
Total Book Value of Preferred Stock:		
Call price (10,0000 × $102)	$1,020,000	
Dividends in arrears (10,000 × 6% × $100)	60,000	$1,080,000
Total Book Value of Common Stock		$475,000

Book Value per Share of Preferred Stock: $1,080,000/10,000 = $108
Book Value per Share of Common Stock: $475,000/97,000 = $4.90

(Treasury stock)

17.

Mihály Company
Income Statement
for the year ended December 31, 19XX

Revenues from Sales			$640,000
Cost of Goods Sold			390,000
Gross Profit			$250,000
Operating Expenses:			
Selling Expenses		$72,000	
General Expenses		67,000	
Total Operating Expenses			139,000
Operating Income			$111,000
Other Income and Other Expenses:			
Gain on sale of equipment		$20,000	
Interest expense		15,000	
Excess Other Income over Other Expense			5,000
Income from Continuing Operations before Income Tax Expense			$116,000
Income Tax Expense on Continuing Operations			34,000
Net Income from Continuing Operations			82,000
Discontinued Operations:			
Operating income from discontinued operations	$26,000		
Less: income tax expense on income from discontinued operations	8,000	$18,000	
Loss from sale of discontinued operations	$13,000		
Less: Tax savings from loss on sale of discontinued operations	4,000	9,000	9,000
Income before extraordinary item			$91,000
Extraordinary item:			
Extraordinary gain		$22,000	
Less: Income tax expense on extraordinary gain		7,000	15,000
Net income			$106,000

17. (*continued*)

Earnings per share:

Income from continuing operations [($82,000-$6,400)/30,000 shares]	$2.52		
Income from discontinued operations ($9,000/30,000 shares)	0.30		
Income before extraordinary item		$2.82	
Extraordinary gain ($15,000/30,000)			0.50
Net income [($106,000-$6,400)/30,000]			$3.32

Computations:

$$EPS = \frac{Income - Preferred\ Dividends}{Command\ Shares\ Outstanding}$$

Preferred dividends: $800 \times 8\% \times \$100 = \$6,400$

Mihály Company
Statement of Retained Earnings
for the year ended December 31, 19XX

Retained earnings, January 1, 19XX, unadjusted	$90,000	
Prior period adjustment-credit	10,000	
Retained earnings, January 1, 19XX, as adjusted	$100,000	
Net income for current year	106,000	
		$206,000
Dividends for current year	14,000	
Retained Earnings, December 31, 19XX	$192,000	$192,000

(Corporate income statement)

Grade Yourself

Circle the numbers of the questions you missed, then fill in the total incorrect for each topic. If you answered more than three questions incorrectly, you need to focus on that topic. (If a topic has less than three questions and you had at least one wrong, we suggest you study that topic also. Read your textbook, a review book, or ask your teacher for help.)

Subject: Corporations: Retained Earnings and Income Statement

Topic	Question Numbers	Number Incorrect
Retained earnings	1, 2, 3, 4	
Stock dividends	5, 6, 12, 13	
Stock split	7	
Fire period adjustment	8	
Treasury stock	9, 10, 14, 15, 16	
Statement of stockholders' equity	11	
Corporate income statement	17	

Also Available

Test Yourself in. . .

American Government

Anatomy & Physiology

Basic Math

Business Calculus

Business Law

College Chemistry

Electric Circuits

Electronic Devices and Circuits

Elementary Algebra

English Grammar

Finite Math

French Grammar

Intermediate Algebra

Introduction to Biology

Introduction to Calculus

Introduction to Data Processing

Introduction to Financial Accounting

Introduction to Managerial Accounting

Introduction to Marketing

Introduction to Psychology

Introduction to Sociology

Organic Chemistry

Physics

Precalculus Mathematics

Principles of Economics (Macroeconomics)

Principles of Economics (Microeconomics)

Spanish Grammar

Statistics

Thermodynamics

Trigonometry

. . . and many others to come!